SUPERCHARGE YOUR DESTINY

AF543281

SUPERCHARGE YOUR DESTINY

Unlock Your Inner Superpowers for a Transformed Life

SWATI TIWARI, PhD

HAY HOUSE INDIA
New Delhi • London • Sydney
Carlsbad, California • New York City

Hay House Publishers (India) Pvt Ltd,
Muskaan Complex, Plot No. 3, B-2, Vasant Kunj, New Delhi 110 070, India
Hay House LLC, P.O. Box 5100, Carlsbad, CA 92018-5100, USA
Hay House UK Ltd, The Sixth Floor, Watson House, 54 Baker Street, London W1U 7BU, UK
Hay House Australia Publishing Pty Ltd, 18/36 Ralph St., Alexandria NSW 2015, Australia

Email: contact@hayhouse.co.in
www.hayhouse.co.in

Copyright © Swati Tiwari 2024

The views and opinions expressed in this book are the author's own and the facts are as reported by her. They have been verified to the extent possible, and the publishers are not in any way liable for the same.

All rights reserved. No part of this publication may be reproduced, by any mechanical, photographic, or electronic process, or in the form of a phonographic recording, nor may it be stored in a retrieval system, transmitted, or otherwise be copied for public or private use – other than for 'fair use' as brief quotations embodied in articles and reviews – without prior written permission of the publisher.

The author of this book does not dispense medical advice or prescribe the use of any technique as a form of treatment for physical, emotional, or medical problems without the advice of a physician, either directly or indirectly. The intent of the author is only to offer information of a general nature to help you in your quest for emotional, physical, and spiritual well-being. In the event you use any of the information in this book for yourself, the author and the publisher assume no responsibility for your actions.

ISBN 978-81-967512-1-0
ISBN 978-81-967512-5-8 (Ebook)

Printed at
Replika Press Pvt Ltd.

FSC www.fsc.org MIX Paper | Supporting responsible forestry FSC™ C016779

This book is produced from FSC® paper to ensure responsible forest management.

To Papa, my first superhero, and Mummy, my biggest cheerleader—you are my North Star.

To Deepak, Shabdita, and Sharanya—you complete me.

To the one who wishes to Evolve, to YOU.

CONTENTS

ACKNOWLEDGEMENTS

From the Deepest Part of My Heart

You, my incredible family, are the foundation on which I stand. This book wouldn't exist without your unwavering support, not just for this project, but for every part of me, always. Thank you for your patience during those early mornings when the lights and noise disrupted our routines. Thank you for understanding my absences, for believing in my dreams and purpose every single time. Your love is the bedrock that allowed this book to rise.

To My Cheerful Crew

My dear friends, your unwavering encouragement pulled me through moments of doubt. Richa, you kept my spirits high and my laughter flowing, reminding me of the joy in the journey. And Monika, your creative writing expertise fine-tuned my introduction in a way I couldn't have managed myself. Thank you!

The Guiding Lights

Omnath, your probing insights and guidance were instrumental in defining the scope of this book and setting it on the right path. I'm immensely grateful for your help.

Sweta Samota, my book writing coach, your expertise and encouragement were instrumental in bringing this project to life.

Binati Sheth, your keen eye for detail and suggestions on chapter titles were a gift. Thank you for helping polish the initial draft.

The Dream Team

To the entire Hay House team, thank you for believing in this project and partnering with me to bring it to life. Your collaborative spirit in refining the title, crafting the perfect cover art, and navigating my edits was invaluable. Your dedication and professionalism are truly inspiring.

Sonali Pawar, my editor at Hay House, whose magic touch made the language sing. You took my manuscript to a whole new level.

The Heart of the Book

My deepest gratitude goes to my amazing coaches and trainees. You entrusted me with your stories, successes, and struggles. Your willingness to share not only fuelled my passion but also shaped the content within these pages. Thank you for your patience during those early days, your belief has been a cornerstone in the creation of this book.

Standing on the Shoulders of Giants

I am forever indebted to the countless gurus and predecessors who have walked this path before me. Their wisdom, shared through books, teachings, and online resources, has been the foundation of my own journey as a coach. Thank you for paving the way and illuminating this path of self-improvement.

THE AWARENESS WITHIN YOU

'For those who have conquered the mind, it is their friend. For those who have failed to do so, the mind works like an enemy.'

—The Bhagavad Gita

Anubhav and Disha were planning to start the 'Candid Cafe' for quite some time. This cafe was the brainchild of Anubhav, a pastry chef, and Disha, a clinical psychologist. Anubhav and Disha finally took a leap, and Anubhav quit his stable job in January 2020. They decided to convert a residential property they owned into their dream cafe, which was set to launch in April 2020. You know what happened next.

Despite preparing for everything, on 24th March 2020, a countrywide lockdown was announced in India for 21 days, courtesy of the Coronavirus Pandemic. They had no job, and all their savings were invested in this cafe. However, the initial 21 days passed, and the lockdown was extended.

Anubhav was in bad shape, feeling stressed, anxious, and irritable. The confinement of being indoors and the inability to earn money led him to drink more than usual, exacerbating his troubles. On the other hand, Disha remained level-headed, thanks to her power of objectivity and honest communication. As a clinical psychologist, she recognised that their future depended on their mindset. She was aware that you first lose in your head. Thus, she had a heart-to-heart with Anubhav and gave him some self-help practices to incorporate into his routine.

Lo and behold, within two weeks of implementing these practices, Anubhav regained control of his life, feeling hopeful and positive once again. He started baking again and launched online delivery options for their cafe. Although initially they envisioned a physical cafe, their positive mindset and adaptability transformed it into a successful cloud kitchen. With an improved mindset, they not only found success but also regained their financial stability!

Another case came my way in 2020. I had an online session scheduled on 'Happiness and Stress Management for Working Professionals' and was getting ready for the same. I wondered if Anubhav and Disha's story was the right example to share with the participants. But things took a turn for the worst. I received a message: 'KUSHAGRA COMMITTED SUICIDE.' This left me numb.

Several questions started running through my mind. How can Kushagra commit suicide? He was successful and had so much to offer to the world. He was living the life people often dream of! He was planning for the future—he had jotted down his goals and dreams meticulously in a journal. Merely a month ago, he recited his bucket list items on our college catch-up Zoom call. This came both as a shock and an eye-opener.

I knew that Kushagra was stressed because of the lockdown and its impact on his personal and professional life. We were all in this state of stress and limbo. Yet Kushagra cracked and succumbed under the pressure.

This was when I resolved to write this book. I realised we cannot approach life in isolation. People are stressed, struggling, and dealing with loneliness, and merely training them on stress management or coping with loneliness wasn't an answer. The targeted sessions were just like treating the symptoms when what we actually needed to do was diagnose the underlying cause. The market already had several programmes designed around these issues. However, I wanted to create a resource focusing on holistic well-being and empowerment, and the result is in your hands!

Always keep in mind that:

> If someone is stressed due to a health issue, then stress can only be managed when their health is taken care of.
>
> If someone is stressed because they cannot get a hold of their finances, then only good financial management can minimise their worries.
>
> If someone is not faring well in their career, then productivity is the only remedy for their stress.
>
> If someone has a strenuous relationship, then the answer to their stress lies within the relationship.

The experiences of both Anubhav and Kushagra were similar, yet their outcomes differed. Their stories are so relatable; they could belong to any of us. Each one of us will have different memories, experiences, struggles, and results. But ask yourself, when life happens, do you drown? Or do you try to stay afloat? What are the forces that make you go under? What is that power that keeps you afloat?

The answer to these questions is your approach. It is also the premise of this book. Your approach—towards this journey called life, which is hard to coach but easy to learn—will always outperform intelligence when it comes to staying afloat, or sinking, in life.

Navigating through life is a skill, and like any other skill, it, too, can be learnt. It's a skill to identify, balance, and use your latent superpowers (or abilities) at the right time and the right place. *Supercharge Your Destiny* uses real and anecdotal short stories to demonstrate these superpowers in action. This book is designed to help you tap into your inner potential and empower you to create the life you want. Within these pages, you'll discover a wide range of superpowers that can be used to transform every aspect of your life. These 40 superpowers are encapsulated under broad topics like 'Financial Wellness', 'Self-Discovery', 'Physical Wellness', 'Patience', 'Outlook', 'Feelings and Emotions', 'Adjustments', 'Conviction', and 'Logic'.

You will also get access to *mantras* to unlock the superpowers that can be developed. Whether you're looking to improve your physical and mental well-being, become more successful and influential, or simply live a more fulfilling and meaningful life, this book is for you.

My intention is to help everyone analyse and tweak their approach to life. Life is not in our control but how we approach life certainly is. Our method determines how we react and respond to life and create wonderful memories.

Supercharge Your Destiny is about holistic empowerment for leading a life of meaningful success and lasting happiness. I offer this complete blueprint to gradually evolve, develop, grow, and improve. The ideas, methods, affirmations, and techniques referred to as mantras—presented here possess the power to turn your life 360 degrees. This book is an attempt to help you evolve consciously—every single day, week, month, and year. It will help you become a better, empowered, 2.0 version of yourself one day at a time.

These tools are effective for everyone, and I say this with great responsibility. I have consciously tried and tested them myself over almost three decades of personal and professional experience. The outcome of *Supercharge Your Destiny* may vary for individuals—some may require more time or effort than others. What works for one person may not be as effective for another. The result depends on various factors such as the current state of your abilities, your natural rhythm, mindset, and, most importantly, the time you dedicate to making changes. Results can vary with each new combination, much like a number lock. If you don't know the passcode, you must consistently experiment with different combinations to discover what works best for you. The focus is on fostering awareness and developing a process.

Key Points to Note as You Read this Book

1. This list of superpowers spelled out in this book is not comprehensive. It's an ever-expanding list.
2. The foundation lies within the psyche rather than the independent functioning of specific brain areas. Moreover, the majority of superpowers exhibit interconnectedness and interdependence.
3. *Supercharge Your Destiny* offers intensely practical pieces of advice. Every chapter has exercises for you. These mantras aim to empower you, but for them to work, you must practise them diligently.
4. The idea is to make this book a habit, a default setting. Discipline and consistency are not optional.
5. This book is meant to enrich your journey and provide memories worth revisiting. Enjoy this journey called life by finding meaning in it.

The secret to achieving a meaningful, successful, and happy life is awareness. Recognise your imperfections, weaknesses, powers, and potential. Be aware of who you are, what you can be, what you want, what you can offer, and what the world needs. Transformation from what you are to what you can be is realised when you find balance and decide to not just exist but also evolve.

How to Read This Book

As awareness takes time, take your time while reading this book and go with the flow. Don't rush through it or skim and scan. I recommend following these steps as you progress through the book:

1. Make an 'Evolve Journal' to jot down the notes and do the exercises. This journal will eventually reflect how far you have progressed.
2. Start with Chapter 1. Read carefully. Reflect. Do the exercises. Reflect again. Once you're happy with what you have learnt, move on to the next chapter.
3. Read the story at the beginning of each chapter. It will ease you into the mindset I want you to focus on.
4. Reflect on the exercise you have been asked to do and record your thoughts in your Evolve Journal.
5. Read the rest of the chapter and understand what it's trying to say.
6. Practise the suggested rituals, exercises and mantras. Introduce one mantra at a time. It will do wonders.
7. Repeat steps 3–6 for each chapter.
8. Don't forget to practise what you've learnt before as you move on to the next chapter. By the end of the book, many of these will become second nature to you.

9. Rinse and repeat. After your first reading is complete, repeat and start over from Chapter 1. Keep adding new reflections and new practices to your daily routine.
10. Incorporate the awareness you gain into your routine practice. Do this daily without fail, but do not over-commit either.

Take a deep breath, turn the page and dive, to claim your superpowers. It's time to evolve.

SUPERPOWER 1

GRATITUDE

Who Packed Your Parachute?

'Lack of gratitude is the greatest sin.'
—Saint Ignatius

It was the 76th mission of his illustrious career. Charles Plumb was flying the aircraft carrier Kitty Hawk during the Vietnam War, when a missile made impact. He ejected from the plane and landed in hostile rival territory where he was captured and spent nearly six years in imprisonment.

Fast forward by 25 years, and Charles Plumb and his wife were enjoying a wonderful evening at a restaurant when a stranger approached them and asked, 'Are you Charles Plumb? Did you fly jets in the Vietnam war? Weren't you shot down?'

Plumb was taken aback, but replied, 'Yes, that's true. But how do you know me? How do you know all these details?'

'I packed your parachute,' the stranger replied with a modest smile.

Plumb was speechless as the stranger shook his hand, and said, 'I am glad it worked! If it hadn't, I wouldn't be here today.'

For obvious reasons, Plumb could not sleep that night. He struggled to remember the stranger. He tried to imagine what he might have looked like in uniform. He wondered how often he had seen him and not even said a 'good morning' or 'how are you?'

How could I miss noticing him? Was it because I was a fighter pilot, and he was just a sailor?

That stranger haunted his thoughts.

How many hours did he spend in the bowels of the ship, standing on that wooden table, carefully folding each parachute for them to work perfectly when needed?

This sailor who held not just a parachute but also the fate of strangers like him in his hands.

This unexpected encounter changed Charles Plumb's life forever. He started travelling as a motivational speaker and told his story to as many people as possible. He always ended his talk by asking, 'Who has packed your parachute?'

Self-Reflection

Get your Evolve Journal to reflect and write the names of people who are packing your parachutes every day, enabling you to lead a comfortable and stress-free life.

Can you imagine doing all this alone?

Did you get where you are without anyone's help?

The first step of this journey is to appreciate and thank everyone who has contributed to your lives, however big or small. Write all the names you remember. If you cannot recall specific names, remember them for their contributions by writing what you identify them with—for instance, their height, skin colour, hair, accent, vehicle colour, etc.

Say thank you to all of them.

Gratitude Is the Ultimate Superpower

As a child, I always felt pity for my friend Rashmi, believing her to be trapped in a conservative society and burdened with a complexion darker than mine. But as we grew up together in our humble neighbourhood, I realised that our circumstances were more similar than I had imagined. I learnt that more than circumstances, our perspective determined our level of contentment with life, defining our fortunes.

One day, I stumbled upon an article that suggested maintain a gratitude journal, and I asked Rashmi to join me in this experiment. Writing down three positive things that happened each day was not easy, especially for Rashmi. Sometimes we reflected together to find things she could be grateful for, however, with time and effort, she also noticed several positive things in her life. Gradually, she became more optimistic and appreciative of the small things.

Witnessing the transformative power of gratitude, I was amazed at the effect this exercise had on Rashmi's mood and relationships. Looking back on this experience, I consider it to be my first life coaching advice, and it opened my eyes to the incredible potential of gratitude to enrich and transform our lives.

The attitude of gratitude is a powerful asset required to evolve. It is an approach that focuses the mind to acknowledge and appreciate things for what they are and become aware of the good things happening with and around you. Follow that up by appreciating everyone involved.

Whether trivial or crucial, learn to be thankful as a routine practice for everything. There is always someone to appreciate and something to be grateful for—good health, wealth, nature, food, business, your job, pets, loving community, etc. The list is never-ending.

I agree that maintaining such an attitude can be difficult during a crisis, making it difficult to see beyond the situation when everything seems pointless. There are moments you take for granted when things are good and everything is normal. You are cherishing the comfort of a regular day, which becomes an everyday thing, making us forget to acknowledge the contribution of factors leading to that blissful existence—the people, nature, or even that supreme power.

Gratitude is a habit; it is the by-product of optimism and abundance. It teaches you to look at all the good things in the world with appreciation. Life is full of surprises—some wonderful, some terrible—but everything is temporary.

Gratitude teaches you to be at peace with yourself. It encourages you to focus on what you have, even in the presence of what you do not. What you focus on grows. A focus on the gratitude attitude gives you more reasons to be happy. You bask in the glow of positivity, improved confidence, and uplifted self-esteem. It is impossible to have it all, however, focusing on what you do have makes you a magnet for more things to be grateful for.

Appreciation of what you already have is the foundation of attracting more abundance. Add more names to your gratitude list. One way to do this is to keep a gratitude journal, just like my childhood friend Rashmi and I did. But if that's not your cup of tea, there are plenty of other practices you can try from the list below. The key is to find a gratitude practice that works for you and that you enjoy. So, go ahead and give it a try, you might just be surprised at how transformative gratitude can be.

Mantras to Unlock an Attitude of Gratitude

1. Gratitude Journal: Bad memories cling to your brain like Velcro, while good memories slip like Teflon. Don't forget to be thankful for the good things. Rewire your brain by consciously reflecting on and recording the things you are grateful for.

   Ask yourself these questions every day:

   'What am I grateful for?'

   'What made me happy?'

   'Who/what all contributed to that happiness?'
2. Set up a Gratitude Jar: Place a gratitude jar for yourself and your family at a noticeable spot. Place a pen and paper next to it. Encourage everyone in your family to log in their moments of gratitude.
3. Gratitude Letter: Write a letter to someone to express your heartfelt gratitude. Posting this letter is optional, but the important thing is to write it. Read your journal, slips in the jar, and these letters on hard days to remind yourself of what you have.
4. Practise Gratitude: Incorporate the 'gratitude attitude' in your daily routine. Make it a habit. Express gratitude every day, and not only on occasions.
5. Start your day with gratitude by saying or writing at least three things you are grateful for. End your day with gratitude by sharing at least three good things that happened during the day with your family or friends. Say, 'I am grateful' and 'thank you' before you sleep.

6. Appreciate Small Things: Don't wait for good things to happen. Express gratitude by consciously looking for things you should appreciate in life. People are chasing after winning. However, in this game of life, we often forget the good things that happen during this game.
7. Develop an active, and not a reactive, gratitude attitude. Slow down. Take a pause to look around. Appreciate all the small things—flowers, rain, sun, friends, your partner, etc.
8. Focus Your Present: be thankful for the present instead of dwelling on the past or stressing about the future. Thank all that you have and all that you have achieved. Take ownership of your present.
9. Expand Your Gratitude Community: Like attracts like. When you are around people filled with gratitude, your mindset will naturally shift. You start focusing on the good things you previously overlooked. Find people with this gratitude mindset, as these are the ones who are grateful and appreciative. Spend time with them, and keep adding such people to your life.
10. Gratitude Meditation: If you feel meditation is difficult and you cannot sit through it, start with gratitude meditation. You can do this anywhere and anytime. Just sit back, relax, close your eyes, and count your blessings. Reflect and thank the events, things, and people you are grateful for.
11. Commit to Practising Gratitude: Make it a daily practice to change your mindset and thought process. Practise gratitude every day, everywhere, and with everyone.

Research suggests that gratitude improves physical, emotional, and social health. It promotes overall well-being (Wood, Linley, and Joseph 2007). As you develop a more positive and grateful attitude, you'll notice more good things coming your way. You will also experience many transformations, sleep better, notice an improved mood, strengthen your relationships, and much more. Be conscious and observe these changes as you follow these practices.

SUPERPOWER 2

OPTIMISM

What Are You Writing On?

'I am not what happened to me; I am what I choose to become.'

—Carl Jung

A blind boy was sitting on a busy street with a hat and a placard that read, 'I am blind. Please help.'

There was hardly any money in the hat when a kind man noticed him. He gave the blind boy some money and asked whether he could change the text on the placard. The boy agreed as he had nothing to lose. With this new text on the placard, many people stopped and gave the blind boy some money.

After a few hours, the man who had changed the text returned and noticed the hat was filled to the brim with money. The blind boy cheerfully asked, 'What did you change?'

The man smiled and said, 'I only changed the approach. It now says: "It's a beautiful day, but I cannot see it."'

Self-Reflection

What would you write on your placard? Reflect and ask yourself, 'What am I worried about at this moment?' If this is about the past, ask, 'Can I change it now?' If it is about the future, ask, 'Can I change it by overthinking?'

Take note of your answers in your Evolve Journal.

Why We Need to Maintain a Positive Attitude

Back in August 2003, I started working at an educational start-up with Pramila and a few others. We were all excited and driven to learn and grow in our careers. But Pramila seemed to be carrying a heavy weight on her shoulders. She complained about her mother-in-law—who always criticised her cooking and interfered in her life—all the time. It was hard to see Pramila so weighed down by her personal issues when the rest of us were focused on our careers.

One day, while we were eating lunch together, Pramila mentioned that she was about to start her *Chaturmaas* (four months) fasting. She typically fasted for four months out of the year and gave up something she loved to eat during that time. Pramila asked us, 'What should I give up for this year's fasting?'

'Why don't you try giving up complaining about your mother-in-law?' I suggested. Pramila's face turned red in embarrassment, and she fidgeted with her hands.

Pramila was hurt and taken aback by my suggestion, but as we talked about it more, she realised that she had developed a habit of complaining about her mother-in-law. This habit was weighing her down and affecting not only herself but also those around her. She would constantly vent to her husband, friends, and colleagues, but it never seemed to make her feel any better.

Despite the initial shock, Pramila decided to take up the challenge and stop complaining about her mother-in-law for her *Chaturmaas* fasting in 2004. As she completed her fast, Pramila realised the transformative power of positive thinking. By avoiding negative thoughts and focusing on the good things in her life, she started to see things differently. Her relationship with her mother-in-law began to improve, and she found herself more content and satisfied. Furthermore, the positive change in Pramila's attitude also impacted her professional life.

Today, Pramila is a successful Dean of Studies at a university. She often talks about how that small shift in her perspective transformed her life for the better. Giving up complaining for her *Chaturmaas* fasting was a turning point that showed her the power of positivity and ways it can impact every aspect of life.

Our brains are hardwired to focus and search for probable threats. We haven't truly evolved beyond our basal survival instincts. This threat-detecting defence mechanism served humankind well when we lived in caves and faced constant danger of being killed. However, the situation has changed. Unfortunately, it seems someone forgot to rewire our brains, as our wiring remains the same. Since we no longer struggle for survival, our minds keep finding threats in pessimism and negativity. This puts both your body and mind in a frayed state of existence. Surely, you don't want that unpleasantness in your life.

Maintaining a positive attitude is not about being positive all the time. It is about defining positivity more broadly. Positivity can be defined as hope or confidence. It is an attitude that makes us say 'this, too, shall pass'. Positivity is the belief and realisation that there is light at the end of the tunnel. During times of struggle, it is a reminder to focus on moments of relief.

A positive attitude enables you to cope with everyday stress more effectively. Positive individuals demonstrate better cognitive and emotional regulation. They are less likely to succumb to addiction. A positive attitude, therefore, impacts the quality of their life.

Be aware of negative self-talk, rumination, blame-game, and magnifying problems. Watch out if you tend to filter and notice the negative on an otherwise beautiful day. Also be aware about certain words like 'always', 'never', and other extreme words. They often serve as red flags, and be conscious when they arise . When you say, 'It always happens to me,' 'I never get anything easily,' reflect and focus on these extreme words. Is what you are thinking really true? Does it really always happen or are you making mountains out of molehills? Does anything good never happens to you or are you victimising yourself?

Get real with yourself. Stop fighting imaginary demons and take control of your emotions. Get real with how your life is instead of how you perceive it to be.

I do realise that fasting is not a right fit for everyone. Don't worry, there are more practices for you to follow to cultivate a positive mindset.

Mantras to Unlock Optimism

1. Separate Imagination and Reality: Most negative self-talk is just thoughts and our imagination, not reality. When you find yourself going down a negativity spiral, stop and write what you are thinking. Then evaluate it rationally. Ask yourself, 'Is this true?' When you see words like 'never', 'ever', 'always', and 'worst', you know they are untrue.

2. Acknowledge a Positive: Focus on the positives. Look at the *one* thing that went right for you on a terrible day. Concentrate on that day. If it seems difficult, then do the previous exercise of writing and separating imagination from reality before acknowledging a positive.
3. Change the Text: Instead of saying, 'I've never done it before,' say, 'It's an opportunity to learn a new skill.' Say, 'I can try to make it work,' instead of saying, 'It's impossible.'
4. Positive Affirmation: Rewire your brain (Murphy 2015) by repeatedly telling it that you can handle the situation. Tell yourself, 'I have the power to control, and the situation is not that bad.'

   Talk to yourself and say, 'I can do it.'
5. Create Self-Affirmations: Coin a personal mantra and recite it to yourself aloud. For example, 'I deserve joy in life,' or 'Everything is in my control.'
6. Humour Helps: Be kind to yourself during a crisis. Do not feel guilty when you smile, laugh, and enjoy yourself on a bad day. Allow yourself to seek humour in everyday life.
7. Go Outdoors: Nature is a great healer. Go out and enjoy the trees, mountains, lakes, rain, birds, and animals. Connect with something, anything and enjoy it.
8. Practise Kindness: Indulge in regular acts of kindness. Even a minor act of kindness like complimenting someone, helping the elderly cross the road, or listening to someone vent helps. You can explore the depths of your kindness in your style.

Once you adapt to a path of positive perspectives, you will find greater happiness in your life. It will empower you to be more productive and better equipped to handle life's surprises.

SUPERPOWER

3

APPRECIATION

Don't Just Say 'Thank You'

'Appreciation can make a day, even change a life. Your willingness to put it into words is all that is necessary.'

—Margaret Cousins

A boy was asked to introduce himself in a job interview without using proper nouns. 'My washerman father raised me with hard work, love, and care. I don't have any memories of my mother as she died during labour,' the boy starts. 'My father made sure I was given the best education. I went to the best public school and after that to the best universities of the country for higher education till my master's degree in management.' He continues, 'I was always the best student in the batch. My father has high hopes that his struggles will finally be over, as I will now take charge of our lives.'

The manager asked, 'You are a brilliant student. You must have received a scholarship and donations to support your studies?'

The boy proudly responded, 'No sir, my entire education was solely taken care of by my father. No scholarship or assistance was available. My father had a tough time. He is a proud man who never asked for anybody's help.'

'That's commendable,' the manager said, 'I am sure you must have shared the load and helped him wash clothes or help out with other household chores.'

The boy replied, 'Never. He always wanted me to focus on my studies. Moreover, he is quicker than I am.'

'I get it,' the manager continued. 'Consider this a part of your job interview. Go back home, clean your father's hands, and see me tomorrow.'

The boy was happy and confident about getting the job. He went back and eagerly asked his father, 'Please extend your hands. I wish to wash them.' His father stretched his hand with a bit of hesitation. The boy started cleaning his father's hands.

For the first time, he noticed his father's sore, wrinkled, and swollen hands. He couldn't help the tears from falling. For the first time, he saw the bruised hands that paid the price for his education, academic excellence, and future. That day, the boy helped his father with everything without saying a word.

The next day, the boy rushed to the manager's office and thanked him for the most valuable lesson he had learnt. With teary eyes, he said, 'If it had not been for this interview exercise, I would have never realised what price my father paid for my well-being. I always knew and acknowledged that he was doing a lot for me, but I could never express it with my words or actions. Now I know what genuine appreciation is.'

The manager said, 'I am glad you realised this. This is what I look for in my team. I want people who don't only recognise and acknowledge, but also genuinely appreciate each other's struggles, efforts, and support. I want people who can empathise and who not only feel gratitude but also express appreciation for each other through their actions and words. You are hired.'

Self-Reflection

Reflect and list some examples or your recent experiences when you felt appreciated, respected, or elevated. Think about these occasions where you felt gratitude and respect for someone. What did you do to express those feelings beyond saying 'thank you'?

As a novice trainer, I was eager to make my mark in the industry. One day, I received a call from the HR manager of Tafe Motors and Tractors Limited. They were looking for a trainer to conduct a four-day training programme for their 250 shop-floor workers and my name had been recommended to them. I was thrilled at the opportunity and readily accepted the offer.

Despite my nerves, my team and I put forth our best efforts and successfully conducted the training programme. The participants were pleased with the programme and several of them acknowledged our effort and approach. However, it was the response of one particular participant that truly stood out to me.

A tall, thin, middle-aged man called Ajeet approached me after the programme with tears in his eyes. He thanked me for the training and said, 'In the last 15 years of my working life, this is the first time I've felt that the company cares. They care about me, how I feel, and what I do.' His response gave me a perspective of how appreciation can go beyond mere words of thanks.

I realised that appreciation and acknowledgement possess incredible potential to transform lives not just in the workplace, but beyond it as well. Ajeet's emotional response to the programme was a testament to this fact. Feeling valued at work boosted his satisfaction, which carried over into his personal life and resulted in an overall improvement in his well-being and relationships—both in and outside of work.

Furthermore, as the trainer in this story, my own sense of fulfilment and purpose was deeply tied to the appreciation I received from Ajeet and the other participants. Although, I didn't expect teary eyes and didn't know how to handle his feelings, they reaffirmed my passion for training and coaching. I felt truly appreciated and surer of the fact that this was my calling. I firmly decided then that training and coaching was going to be my life's work.

This experience showed me that the power of appreciation goes beyond just words of thanks and the immediate benefits for the recipient. It has a transformative effect on both the person giving and receiving the appreciation. Since then, I have consciously made a few changes in my approach, such as I try to be more expressive, I appreciate more, and I do not get offended easily.

Today, I firmly believe that appreciation is a powerful force that can transform lives. By taking the time to acknowledge and express gratitude for the people and things that matter to us, we create a ripple effect of positivity that can extend far beyond just work.

You would agree with me that we need more appreciation in this world. All of us long for appreciation. Showing others you appreciate them is imperative. Appreciation is often confused with a simple thank you or praise, however, it goes beyond just words. It is about valuing abilities, skills, personas, and the uniqueness in people. Appreciation relates to physical beauty, crafts, talents, excellence, and moral beauty in individuals.

Both appreciation and gratitude are often confused and used interchangeably (Watkins 2013). Although are conscious positive emotions, gratitude is about acknowledging what others have done for us—tangibly or intangibly. On the other hand, appreciation is more about the present moment. It is about being actively aware of reflecting on what you feel, of knowing that you are grateful, and of understanding why you are thankful. You can feel gratitude for having access to two square meals every day, while appreciation goes beyond and focuses on the taste, colour, nutrition value, and the efforts gone into preparing and cooking that meal.

Genuine appreciation is the most basic need in both private and professional lives. Nothing in this world drives and engages humans more than appreciation and nothing else can substitute the feeling of: 'I truly matter. I have the ability to contribute. I am recognised for what I do.'

Appreciation is the most sought-after superpower. It lifts us, energises us, and brings out the best within us. Somehow, we find it awkward to appreciate and praise someone freely but are quick to point out mistakes and discouraging others. In many ways, unfortunately, we have mastered the art of expressing negative emotions and not learning to express our positive emotions comfortably. It's important to start practising appreciation now, and you can do so with the exercises mentioned below.

Mantras to Unlock Appreciation

1. Don't be Picky: Appreciate small things, and don't wait for only big things to happen to practise appreciation. Appreciation is a habit, and it is developed once you realise there's nothing too small to appreciate.
2. Appreciate Yourself: If it's difficult for you to appreciate others, then chances are you find it difficult to appreciate yourself as well. Begin with appreciating yourself. Reflect upon each day to locate why—and for what—you should feel proud of yourself today. You can also plan for the next day. Say, 'What do I plan to do tomorrow to feel proud of?'
3. Resolve to Harm Less: When we point out others' mistakes and discourage them, it harms them. Resolve to hurt people less. Use these negative emotions within your heart to locate the root cause of your insecurity. Don't project your emotions onto others and unintentionally hurt them.
4. Notice the Positive: Everyone has positive qualities. We either ignore or take them for granted. Consciously strive to notice others' positive behaviours, qualities, and contributions. Strive to see the unique qualities of people around you.
5. Be Expressive: When you convey your appreciation, people around you are also inspired to do so. In such an environment, people feel comfortable easily expressing their positive emotions.
6. Spend More Time with Loved Ones: Spending time with someone you love and care about is a sign that you enjoy and appreciate their company. It also helps you grow closer and have a better chance at noticing and appreciating their positive qualities.

7. Be Easy to Impress: Everyone in this world is incredible and full of miracles. Don't be arrogant and say things like, 'I already know this,' or 'What's the big deal?' don't help. In fact, when you are impressed quickly, you feel positive and energised. This positivity builds stronger relationships and an optimistic approach to life.
8. Be Hard to Offend: Alongside being easy to impress, grow a thicker skin to enhance your appreciation for life. Don't take anything personally—most things are not about you. Moreover, nobody has the power to offend you without your permission.
9. Engage with Beauty: Take some time out every day to describe the beauty you witnessed that day. Firstly, notice the beauty of nature. Secondly, observe the man-made beauty. Lastly, tune into the beauty of people's behaviour.

We often talk about appreciation from the recipient's point of view, but know that there are plenty of benefits for the giver as well. Appreciate freely. Venture into the realm of treasuring and cherishing the world around you with open arms.

SUPERPOWER 4

HOPE

Did You Calibrate Your Compass?

'If you knew that hope and despair were paths to the same destination,
which would you choose?'
—Robert Brault

A man was running heavy losses in his business. As a last resort, he sold his property to fund the company. One day, his son asked, 'Why are you selling our property and funnelling so much money in this loss-making business? Why don't you shut down this business?'

The businessman smiled at his son's impatience, and replied, 'For hope.'

His son haughtily responded, 'What is this hope? And how can it help?'

This back-and-forth carried on for some time.

The son was adamant and the father wanted to instil a sense of hope in his son. So, he decided to illustrate the lesson of hope in another way.

One fine day, he took his son to a well and asked him to jump.

'I don't know how to swim!' resisted the son, 'How can you ask me to jump in a—'

Before he could complete his question, his father pushed him and hid.

The son struggled and tried hard to stay afloat. He was exhausted within five minutes and started drowning. This was when his father pulled him out.

The next day, his father took him to the well again and asked him to jump. Initially, the boy hesitated, but then he took the plunge, and his father went into hiding again.

He struggled, just like the day before. However, this time, he pushed harder and kept floating for over fifteen minutes before exhaustion took over.

At that point, his father pulled him out of the well, and asked, 'What was different today? How did you manage floating longer today?'

He replied, 'Yesterday, when you pushed me, I didn't know what to do. I was afraid. Today, I knew you were there and would save me before I drowned.'

'This is hope, my son.'

Self-Reflection

Visualise where you want to be one year, five years, and ten years from now. Sketch a pathway to reach these goals.

Hope Is the Guiding Compass of Life

I once received a call from an excited yet humble voice, 'Hi Coach, I am Rashid. I wanted to thank you.'

Rashid explained that he had attended my life-changing session sponsored by his employer a few years back. Though he listened to what I had to say, he didn't think it would make a noticeable difference in his life. It was last year when he was going through a rough patch in life that he, fortunately, stumbled upon the notes on developing active hope he took during the session.

Rashid mentioned that he had nothing to lose, so, decided to give it a try. He started with a hope audit, examining the areas of his life that needed improvement and setting goals for himself. He then began journalling, putting his thoughts and feelings down on paper to gain clarity and perspective. Finally, he started meditating to finding peace and stillness within himself.

'These practices were a game changer,' Rashid exclaimed. As he continued with these practices, he began to feel a sense of control and optimism about the future. He knew that he would still face challenges, but at least now he had a compass of active hope to overcome them. He compared using these practices to using a compass with an anchor, ensuring that he was pointed in the right direction and firmly rooted in the present moment.

Rashid called me to express his gratitude and said that he never would have thought that a simple weekend session would have such a profound impact. His experience is a proof to the power of cultivating active hope and several ways it can transform one's life during difficult times.

Is the glass half-full or half-empty? It is half-full if you have hope. Hope is a superpower. It spearheads our sense of possibility. It helps define optimistic expectations for the future and positivity in the present. It involves hopefulness and an eye for good things coming your way. Hope strengthens you when things are not going as planned. It is that motivation and confidence that says goals can be reached, hurdles can be overcome, and new effective avenues can be found to attain the desired future. With hope, life has seemingly endless potential.

Hope is believed to evolve from a position of weakness and is considered the last resort. It is assumed to be explored when we run out of ideas and is perceived to be the light at the end of the tunnel. However, it is more than that.

Hope is more important than ever when things feel impossible. But hope is also much more than a passive act. It is not reactive. It is not something that should be turned to only when you are in the midst of a dark, bottomless pit. Hope is not a magical switch that flicks on when you are waiting for a miracle. Hope is a lifestyle, as it defines what you do and who you are. It is you and the tunnel—before entering the tunnel, while walking the tunnel, and after exiting the tunnel.

When used proactively, hope builds self-confidence and self-belief (Gordon 2011). It keeps one motivated and reduces misery, anxiety, fear, and stress. Hope fuels the sense of control and optimism. Together, optimism and hope foster happiness and well being. However, to reap all the physical, mental, and social benefits of this superpower, you must first adopt a mindset and perspective of hope.

As you journey through life, it is important to remember that hope is your compass, guiding you towards your goals and helping you navigate the challenges you may face along the way.

Mantras to Unlock Hope

1. Hope Audit: Conduct a hope audit for yourself. How are you doing at work? In relationships? In health? In finance?
2. Practise Gratitude: Acknowledge your existence and be thankful for what you have. Before starting your day, make sure to practise gratitude by thanking everyone and everything that makes your life worth living.
3. Keep a Journal: Every night before going to bed, in your Evolve Journal, write down at least three things that went well during the day.
4. Set Goals: Write down goals for yourself—for today, for tomorrow, for one year, two years, and ten years from now. What do you want to be? How do you want to reach there? Where do you want to go? Ask all the questions you'd like to be asked about your present and your future.
5. Develop Belief Systems: Paint a vivid image of your topmost goals. Visualise your best possible self in relation to this goal. What will your goals look like? What would you experience in the moment you achieve them? Envision the possible pathways to your goals, major probable roadblocks, and define strategies to navigate these problems.
6. Reflect on Past Successes: Keep your positive emotions alive and ponder upon the small and big successes of both the recent and distant pasts. This will keep you optimistic, reassuring you that things are fine and will be fine in the future as well.
7. List Your Strengths and Resources: In terms of your most important goals, list the strengths and resources you

already have. Then plan your action for the skills and resources you lack.

8. Develop Coping Skills: What is your pain point—time management, stress management, or procrastination? Acknowledge your weaknesses, and then develop skills to cope with them to strengthen yourself.
9. Spend Time with Hopeful People: Your success is defined by the average of the five people with whom you spend the most time. When you spend time with hopeful people, you soak yourself in that positive environment and encourage yourself to be hopeful, too.
10. Find Humour: Humour keeps hope alive. Find the comedy in existence to laugh and loosen up a little.
11. Do What You Can: Keep moving when you are in despair, as taking one extra step can make all the difference. Make your bed, talk to a friend, or cook a healthy meal. Once you're done with that one step, add another step. This will break the inertia of helplessness.
12. Adjust Your Focus: Concentrate on things that are in your control and on people who empower you. Stop endlessly ruminating on a problem and thinking about what's not working. This will put you in a better position.
13. Perform an Act of Kindness: An act of kindness triggers the release of happiness-inducing hormones like dopamine, serotonin, endorphins, and oxytocin.
14. Enhance Your Wellness: Eat healthy, stay hydrated, exercise regularly, take good rest, and practise mindfulness and meditation.

With these simple everyday practices, you can calibrate your compass and develop the superpower of hope that is active, not reactive. This compass will keep you steady on your way to leading a meaningful life. Stay hopeful, be positive, and progressively set goals.

SUPERPOWER

5

HUMOUR

What Would Birbal Do?

'A person without a sense of humour is like a wagon without springs. It's jolted by every pebble on the road.'

—Henry Ward Beecher

A man was running late one day. He was driving above the speed limit. Suddenly, in the rear-view mirror, he noticed a police vehicle following him.

He thought that he could lose them, so he floored the accelerator. Now, both vehicles were racing on the city streets at a high speed. Finally, as his speedometer reached 80 km/hr, the man thought he couldn't do it anymore on these narrow streets and gave up. He pulled over to the curb.

The police officer was furious. As he approached the speeding car, he held the man by the collar and said, 'Listen, mister, I've had a long day, and I just want to go home. Give me one good reason, and I'll let you go.'

With some hesitation, the man thought for a moment and replied, 'My wife escaped three weeks ago with a police officer. When I saw you chasing me, I thought you were that same officer, and you now want to give her back to me!'

They both eased into their cars and drove away.

Self-Reflection

Think about a stressful experience from your recent past. How did you resolve the situation? Was it solved in a humorous manner? How could you have solved it humorously? When did you last laugh at yourself?

Humour Is Serious Business

At a weekend session that I was facilitating, I came across a participant named Manoj who appeared serious all the time. He never laughed at the jokes, and he always wore a poker face. I could also see that he was having trouble connecting with the other participants.

After the session, I approached Manoj to strike up a conversation. I asked him if he was ready to take part in an experiment. He replied that he had never been a people person and that he could take part in the experiment if it was not going to be a group activity. I told him that the experiment was simple, and he just had to watch some comedy shows on Netflix that were on our list.

At first, Manoj was taken aback. He informed me he had never been interested in comedy and that he didn't think he could ever find the genre funny. However, he still agreed as he had already committed. I told him to keep an open mind and reflect on his reactions. I also asked him to keep me posted on his reactions and reflections from time to time.

A week later, I received an e-mail from Manoj. He had watched the comedy shows and was surprised to find himself laughing out loud. He mentioned that he had never experienced such light-hearted and carefree. He mentioned that he had never before experienced such light-heartedness and carefreeness. After this, I asked him if he wanted to continue with the experiment, and he agreed. This time, I instructed him to observe funny people around him while continuing to watch more comedy shows. I also asked him to reflect on his feelings when people were being funny.

Two weeks later, Manoj not only appreciated humour but even started practising telling jokes with his friends and family. His e-mail read, 'While I didn't always get a laugh, I am enjoying this.'

This time I asked him to reflect on and appreciate irony while continuing to hone his amateur jesting skills. During our follow-up discussion sessions, Manoj surprised everyone when he said, 'I've been thinking a lot about my sense of humour, and I've come to the conclusion that I'm just not cut out for some things. Like, have you ever tried to teach a fish how to climb a tree? That's me trying to joke!'

The group chuckled, and Manoj's self-deprecating humour helped to lighten the mood. Everyone appreciated his willingness to poke fun at himself, which made him more relatable to the group.

After a month, Manoj was different. He was more welcoming, and his sense of humour made him more approachable. He had cultivated a sense of humour that he never knew he had within him, and I felt proud to have played a small part in his journey.

I grew up listening to countless humorous folk tales about the Mughal emperor Akbar and his ingenious advisor Birbal, who could solve any problem with his wit and humour. Even though it was the way of life then, unfortunately, these days, I don't see many people using humour, cracking jokes, or proving their point with wit like Birbal. Humour has become a privilege awarded to the comics rather than it being a way of life.

Tasteful humour can be the key to success. We have successfully used it in the past. Humour is a superpower that strengthens relationships, defuses tension, aids creativity, boosts confidence, bolsters resilience, and eases pain during trying times.

Humour defines the culture, and culture defines humour. In cultures that encourage people to be themselves, people are more confident with their humour. In such a relaxed environment where humour is second nature, even those who aren't comfortable sharing their limericks can take a chance.

In the current zeitgeist, as a community, we take ourselves way too seriously and have become intolerant. Even witty people have to tone down the edge of their humour as they fear offending somebody. We also fear not being perceived as funny individuals. This unwillingness to take a joke doesn't set the ball rolling. Whatever your reason may be, when you and people around you find it difficult to be funny, take charge and diffuse the situation with some amusing moments.

This does not imply that everyone should be a stand-up comic, we must simply give humour a chance. Well-placed humour always enhances one's quality of life, as it is a proven stress buster, a much-needed armour. It helps break through tense situations and eases the environment, where people can be more productive. Humour helps build trust and morale. Witty individuals are simple to approach, making communication and relationships easier.

Humour is a great leveller. When you find common ground to laugh together, everyone is more likely to forget the power difference and consider each other as equals.

Mantras to Unlock Humour

1. Don't Be Silly: There is a difference between being funny and being humorous. Funny people are good at making timely jokes and narrating fun-filled stories. Being funny is about making others laugh, and being humorous is about taking a joke. Humorous people are accessible, as they don't take anything seriously—they can laugh at anything. Sense of humour is a superpower as it enables you to see the absurdities of life. You don't need to be funny to be humorous. You don't have to crack silly jokes. You simply need to enjoy and encourage good humour.
2. Understand Where Humour Can Be Helpful: Use humour to cheer people up and build rapport. Humour can make your speech more enjoyable, as it makes the message more memorable.
3. Appreciate Irony: Appreciate humour. The first step to learning any skill is to start appreciating it and developing an understanding of it. Laugh at the jokes cracked about you and stay positive.
4. Practise Finding Humour: To develop humour, practise looking at the funny side of otherwise ordinary situations, events, and people. There is a fun side to almost everything.
5. Observe Humorous People: Spend time with people you think are humorous and observe them. How do they have

a different perspective towards life? Pay attention, and if possible, contribute by exchanging banter with them.

6. Find Your Funny Bone: What makes you laugh? Do you laugh at people, situations, events, life's imperfections, differences, or commonalities? Find your natural place.
7. Don't Overdo It: In an attempt to be humorous, avoid being mean. Refrain from overdoing your jokes to demean, offend, or upset others.
8. Surprise Is Safe Humour: Do or say something unexpected to surprise people and create a light mood.
9. Be Spontaneous: Many fear the joke not working or looking like a fool when their joke flops. With a healthy sense of humour, you understand that it's okay to look stupid. Don't overthink your attempt to be humorous. It will make you more confident and natural at humour.

Humour can prove to be a superpower both at work and in life (Aaker and Bagdonas 2020). Practise these mantras and wear the armour of humour because laughter is the best defence against stress and negativity. Humour can do wonders when practised right. It will make you unstoppable by inculcating courage, creativity, and resilience.

SUPERPOWER 6

SOCIAL INTELLIGENCE

Are You Likeable?

'When I get ready to talk to people, I spend two thirds of the time thinking what they want to hear and one third thinking about what I want to say.'

—Abraham Lincoln

One day, a father cooked some rice for dinner, served it in two bowls, and placed it on the dining table. He then called his son, 'Come, Arjun, let's have dinner.'

Arjun came running. His father asked him to choose his bowl. Both bowls had rice, but in one bowl an egg was placed carefully over the rice. Arjun chose the bowl with the egg. He was happy with his choice. But shortly, he was disappointed because his father's bowl had two eggs hidden under the rice. Arjun regretted making his choice in a hurry.

His father then spoke, 'Son, always remember, whatever is visible to the eyes may not be the whole truth.'

The next day, the father called Arjun for dinner. The table was set exactly as it had been the day before, with two bowls of rice—one with an egg on top and the other without. Arjun was asked to pick his bowl, and as he had learnt, he picked the bowl without the egg on top. Arjun started eating his dinner in anticipation of the hidden eggs, but to his surprise, there were none to be found!

His father smiled and said, 'Your past experiences can guide you sometimes, but they can also mislead you. Be prepared, for life may have all sorts of surprises in store.'

On the third day, the rice-and-egg routine was repeated. Arjun was called to choose his bowl, but this time, he deferred the choice. Instead, he told his father, 'Dad, you are elder to me. You are the one who has put in the effort to make this meal. You choose first.'

The father graciously picked up the bowl with an egg on top, and then both began to eat. Arjun was certain that there were no eggs in his bowl. To his surprise, he found two eggs in his bowl. His father, proud and overwhelmed by Arjun's approach, said, 'Son, always remember, when you wish and care for the good of others, good happens to you.'

Self-Reflection

Sit back, relax, and reflect. Imagine yourself at a party where you hardly know anyone. Reflect on how comfortable or awkward you feel there. Are you sitting in a corner or moving around? Do you strike up a conversation, or do you wait for another person to start it? Are people around you comfortable? How do you make them feel? How many new connections do you establish once the party is over?

Do You Want to Be Socially Intelligent?

My client Jhanvi was struggling both personally and professionally. She often found herself in arguments and debates, which led to conflict and tension in her relationships. During our coaching sessions, we discovered that her lack of social intelligence was getting in the way of her growth. She was constantly trying to prove her point instead of listening to others and appreciating their perspectives.

Together, we worked on developing her social intelligence by practising active listening, asking questions to understand others' perspectives, and withholding arguments. With time and dedication, Jhanvi began to appreciate the value of diversity and differences and realised that this was what made the world a more interesting and dynamic place.

Jhanvi is now a successful entrepreneur and has a beautiful, understanding family. Jhanvi's success story is a validation of the power of self-reflection, dedication, and practise.

Social intelligence is a superpower as it helps establish and maintain relationships. It is about communicating with empathy and being assertive with people—the ones you already know and the ones you do not. Social intelligence involves accurately perceiving the motives and emotions of both oneself and others, and adapting effectively to a social environment. It entails knowing what to do or say, when to say or do it, and how to communicate effectively. Research suggests that the most likeable people have high social intelligence (Carnegie 2016).

Socially intelligent people are inherently self-aware, a quality that helps them make and maintain their rapport. Their presence is undeniable, as they radiate confidence even in crowded environments. They are also active listeners, who communicate with sincerity and prefer discussions over arguments. Furthermore, they excel as team players, a trait that translates well into effective management. Their adaptability to evolving emotions, situations, and contexts makes them not only more productive as individuals but also more adept at navigating interpersonal dynamics.

Whether you are comfortable or not, you are always in a social setting—be it your personal, professional, or social life. Social intelligence is the highway to success, an unstoppable road that can get you anywhere you wish. Conversely, lacking social intelligence can hinder your progress, regardless of your capabilities.

If you're struggling with social intelligence, it's important to recognise that it can be developed over time with the right mindset and approach. By practising techniques that suit your temperament, you, too, can become a more socially intelligent and empathetic person.

Mantras to Unlock Social Intelligence

1. Withhold an Argument: While an argument may secure victory in a discussion, it can also hurt the other party or team. Give the situation another thought before reacting impulsively in the heat of the moment.
2. Be Observant: Pay close attention to the people around you. Notice their expressions, moods, and manner of speaking. Everything around us is dynamic, however, we often stay in autopilot. We seldom take the initiative of morphing ourselves according to different social settings. Observe socially intelligent people and learn from their mannerisms. See if their methods work for you, and keep trying till you find your social rhythm.
3. Follow Your Instincts: Humans are perceptive, and have the ability to understand and perceive the world around them. The emotional variations in any social setting aid in understanding the vibe. When you feel strongly—either

positivity or an unusual discomfort—in the presence of an individual, stop and reflect. Try to understand the 'what' and 'why' behind your instinct.

4. Respect Differences: We are all different in many ways and should strive to recognise what distinguishes each of us. This can be achieved by considering perspectives shaped by factors such as culture, region, religion, age, gender, etc., within the conversation.
5. Listen Actively: Listen to comprehend, not just to reply. Notice the words, tone, volume, emotions, and physicality. Try to perceive the undertones alongside the overtones. Stay focused, ask questions to clarify ambiguity, do not interrupt the speaker, encourage the speaker, and focus on non-verbal cues.
6. Show that You Care: Strive to pay attention to the emotions of the people who matter to you. Show them love and care. When people around you are upset, lend them an ear and reassure them of your presence when they need support.
7. Appreciate Others: Don't take people for granted, especially those who love you. Recognise their efforts. Chant this mantra to yourself: 'If you love it, say it.'
8. Focus on the Positives: When people hurt you, look for at least one positive element in their behaviour. Ask yourself: 'Is this behaviour temporary or situational?' or 'Is it the nature of that person?'

Society is becoming complex with each passing day. Developing social intelligence requires practise. To reset your default settings, expose yourself to vulnerable situations. Take control of the situation and learn self-analysis. Make some effort in learning how to act.

[illegible] — in the [illegible] [illegible] [illegible] who will respect your influence.

4. [illegible] We attend different meetings, [illegible]

5. [illegible]

6. [illegible]

7. [illegible] that person?

[illegible]

SUPERPOWER 7

HUMILITY

To Err Is Human

'Humility is not thinking less of yourself, it's thinking of yourself less.'

—C. S. Lewis

A celebrated pandit lived in India around 900 years ago. He could answer every question posed to him. He had travelled the length and breadth of the country to prove his mettle. He challenged the most prominent scholars, thinkers, philosophers, and mystics to debate him. He dominated every single debate to the extent that other scholars refused to challenge him to protect their reputations. Intellectuals started avoiding him. His fame spread far and wide. Furthermore, he also amassed a lot of wealth.

One day, he entered a town on a decked palanquin carried by four strong men. There was mayhem in town. Scholars ran away to escape the challenge. A random voice from behind said, 'Sir, Can I ask you a question?'

The pandit waved his hand to call the challenger ahead, 'Who is this Braveheart who does not fear public humiliation?'

A five-year-old boy stood in front of Panditji, looked him straight in the eyes, and asked again, 'Sir, can I ask you a question?'

'Is it some kind of joke? I am a champion scholar of the world. Get away!' the pandit sneered, and kept moving.

'But I have a question for you,' the child repeated.

The irritated pandit barked, 'You are hardly out of your cradle. Do you even know what debate is? Debating is serious business. Get out, now!'

'When you know everything, why can't you answer just one question?' the child insisted, 'my age and size don't really matter.'

Panditji relented, 'Okay, go ahead and ask your question.'

The child pulled up a handful of sand and asked, 'How many grains of sand are in my hand?'

Panditji was bowled over. For the first time in his life, he had no answer. The child's rendering him speechless quickly became news, attracting a gathering of people eager to see what would happen next.

The wise child preached, 'Sir, any amount of knowledge is a waste if you cannot see the reflection of God in everyone. Scholars should be like a tree bearing fruits that bows down. If one cannot respect others, their knowledge becomes like this hand full of sand—worthless,' and then the child threw the sand away.

Coming from a five-year-old, this hit the pandit to the core of his heart. He was embarrassed but awake. He came down from his palanquin, bowed down at the child's feet, and with humility in his voice, said, 'Please, accept me as your disciple.'

This five-year-old was Parashara—from the twelfth century—the immediate successor of the great Indian philosopher Ramanujacharya.

Self-Reflection

Reflect on your past. Visit a local vegetable or fruit seller. Think of your gestures, posture, body language, words, and tone as you interact with them. Did you bargain? Did you raise your voice? Take note. Conversely, visit a luxury hotel. Reflect on your gestures, posture, body language, words, and tone. Did you bargain? Did you raise your voice? Take note.

Compare your reactions. Was there a difference in your approach at both the places? Make sure to reflect on the 'why'. At work, think about your behaviour with your superiors and your juniors.

Do You Make Room for Humility?

Humility is often the most underrated superpower. Despite its importance being mentioned significantly in religious texts, it is considered a weakness in modern times (Roy 2013). People associate humility with low self-esteem, lower self-opinion, and a lack of confidence. In fact, humility is about possessing enough confidence and self-assurance to say, 'I am good, but I can be better. Someone else can also be better than me, and even if they aren't, I don't need to brag about my goodness.'

In December 2017, I landed an incredible opportunity—three modules, six days, and two corporate clients in Maharashtra. It was a dream come true for my training and life-coaching business, CatchUp Consultants. We were on cloud nine. My reputation as a full-time corporate trainer and life coach was growing, and I was basking in the glory of successful training programmes, satisfied clients, rave reviews, and repeat businesses. My schedule was jam-packed, and I was proud of my decision to leave my old job and pursue my dream of training and coaching.

The first two days went smoothly with a group of humble textile company employees. They appreciated our training, and we basked in their applause and praise. I felt invincible.

But then came the highly qualified and experienced IT company employees. Training was second nature to them, but I just couldn't seem to meet their expectations. They gave us a series of bad reviews, complaining that our programme was ineffective. I was shocked and embarrassed. I made excuses, blaming the participants and the organisation's environment for the lacklustre performance.

But the third day was a wake-up call. I had no more excuses. I was disappointed in myself and began to doubt my abilities as a trainer. I had to take a step back and analyse what had gone wrong. That's when I realised that my past quick wins had made me overconfident and complacent. I had started to believe that I was blessed with immense talent and skills, leading me to not prepare and practise as much. I knew I had to change.

I humbled myself and accepted that even if I were the best—which I certainly wasn't—there was always room for improvement. I needed to stay grounded, focused, and put in the effort to deliver quality training programmes. This realisation hit early on, and I was grateful for it.

I quickly got back on track. Instead of pretending to have all the answers, I started asking more questions, acknowledging the greatness in others, listening more attentively, and admitting when I didn't know something. By being humble, I was able to build deeper and more meaningful relationships with my clients. They trusted me more, and my business continued to grow.

Thus, a coach's journey is not just about training others, but also about the willingness to stay humble and work hard to learn and grow as an individual. While receiving bad reviews was difficult, they taught me an invaluable lesson in humility and helped me become not only a better trainer and coach but a better person.

Humility is self-awareness about your abilities, talents, strengths, flaws, and weaknesses without any arrogance or low self-esteem. Humility is acknowledging and learning from your errors and recognising your weaknesses. Humility is appreciating feedback instead of getting defensive. It is the sense that the best can err. Humility plays a significant role in self-improvement and holistic well-being, as people who are humble are eager to learn and improve, providing them an edge over others.

Mantras to Unlock Humility

1. Ask Questions: People who lack humility often find it difficult to ask questions. They also struggle with asking for help. Don't shy away from asking questions, thinking that it may portray you to be a weak person. In fact, they make you stronger—both mentally and physically.
2. Appreciate People: Recognise and genuinely appreciate people for their achievements. When you do so, the spotlight should be on them, not you. You will be required to shift your focus from yourself to them. Appreciate people who practice humility, as this builds an environment for others to be the same.

3. Give and Receive Feedback: Give verifiable and controllable feedback to people as well as accept feedback with an open mind and heart.
4. Build Confidence: Humility comes from confidence. Whenever you feel you lack confidence, dress up nicely. Make it a daily practise regardless of whether you are stepping out or not. Reflect on your past achievements and the hardships you have faced.
5. Mind Yourself: There are moments in everyone's life when they feel proud of their achievements. People praise us and quote our examples, and no doubt it feels good to be validated. However, mind your words and actions in these moments. Ask yourself, 'Am I acting like a snob?' 'Are my words hurtful?' be honest to yourself.
6. Watch your Ambition: Are you ambitious for the world or just yourself? To stay humble, look beyond the self and focus on a larger purpose like an organisation, society, or your nation (Collins and Collins 2001).

Remember to stay humble and not let ego get in the way of achieving great things. Keep your strengths in check and use them in a positive way. Don't let them control you or lead you into making poor decisions. Humility can help you stay motivated and focused as well as building strong relationships with others. By staying humble, you can learn to be the best version of yourself from others and work with them towards a larger goal.

SUPERPOWER 8

EMPATHY

Where Does the Shoe Bite?

'The greatest cruelty is our casual blindness to the despair of others.'

—Anonymous

A little girl went to the kennel in the neighbourhood and asked the owner, 'Can I have a puppy?'

'Child, you are too young to take care of these little ones,' the owner said. 'Have you asked your parents?'

'No, but I promise I will take care of them,' she pleaded. 'Please give me one.'

To discourage the girl, the owner said, 'I sell them for a lot of money. Do you have any?' Disheartened, the child went home but came back with a piggy bank in her hand.

'There are a lot of coins that I have been saving in this piggy for years. Take them all,' she confidently said, 'now can I have one?'

Flattered by her innocence, the owner said, 'Okay, dear, come with me and choose your puppy.' He then whistled and called the mother dog, 'Come, Chinku!'

She came running with her five adorable puppies. The child's excitement was clear from her broad smile. Her eyes started dancing in delight when she noticed another puppy limping towards them, struggling to catch up with his siblings.

'I want that one!' she shouted with a thrill.

The kennel owner said, 'He is disabled. He can never run and play with you like other dogs.'

The little girl was silent for a while. Then she pulled her jeans up to show her prosthetic leg. 'I also don't run too well myself. I will need one who understands.'

The kennel owner's heart was full. Without saying a word, he picked up the pup and placed it on her lap.

Self-Reflection

Reflect on how effortless or complicated it is for you to understand people who are different from you. The difference could be age, gender, situations, perspectives, fortunes, financial or educational status, moods, capabilities, or anything else. Think about how comfortable you are walking in their shoes. Take note of all these reflections in your evolve journal.

Empathising with Others

My clients, Meenu and Rajesh, had come to me seeking relationship counselling. They had been struggling to connect lately, and their disagreements seemed to be getting more frequent and intense. They were fighting about almost everything from the cleanliness of the house to what was for dinner and whether their children would go for tuition. Their fights were pointless, but the tension in the house was affecting their children. One of the main points of contention was Rajesh's lack of regular income, which left Meenu feeling burdened with the responsibility of supporting their household.

During our sessions, both Meenu and Rajesh expressed their frustrations with each other, and I noticed that they were stuck in a cycle of blaming each other and not truly understanding each other's perspectives. To break this cycle, I suggested an empathy-building exercise of 'taking perspective' where both were asked to reflect on how a neutral third party—who wants the best for all—would view the conflict in their relationship. They were then supposed to take notes and reflect as a couple.

At first, they were hesitant, and it was difficult for them to see things differently. But with some inquiring and intervention, Richa started taking the perspective of her husband's experiences as an entrepreneur. She realised that her husband was passionate about his business and was consistently supporting her with household chores, even though it wasn't in the form of a regular income. Rajesh did his part, too. He was now aware of the stress that Richa was feeling, and he acknowledged that he needed to be mindful while spending or investing in the business.

After a few sessions, during individual sessions, I asked Meenu to take another exercise and imagine her life without Rajesh. She was intrigued to picture this clearly. She was asked to reflect on her feelings, notice the impact of what this would be like, and how different would be her life.

Rajesh was finding this exercise difficult, so I asked him to write a love letter. He was asked to think about his love for Meenu and write down his feelings in the form of a letter. He was also asked to link his thoughts and feelings to something that took place recently. Sharing this letter with Meenu was not necessary for the exercise but he complied.

These empathy-building exercises helped them find common ground and communicate effectively. By putting themselves in each other's shoes and understanding each other's perspectives, Meenu and Rajesh were able to break free from their cycle of blame and work towards a more fulfilling and satisfying relationship. Now when they work together, I feel a sense of pride as they have found a way to find solutions to their problems and make joint decisions on finances and other aspects of their lives.

Empathy is a superpower that helps you understand others' emotion(s) in an appropriate manner. It is the ability to feel what others are feeling and enables you to understand *why* they are feeling so. Empathy is the foundation of compassion, kindness, and love. Essentially, it is like putting your feet in another person's shoes and walking their walk. Where does the shoe bite? How painful is the bite? Is there any solution to this pain?

A 2017 study conducted by Steve Browne suggests that empathetic individuals build connections quickly and are better managers and workers. They also form better connections with family and friends. Empathetic people also understand their own emotions more clearly, which aids in regulating the situation and managing stressful conditions appropriately. The world is a reflection of the self. When you understand and help others, they, too, empathise with you.

It is not an exaggeration to say that this superpower of empathy can ensure everyone's happiness and well-being. However, here's a word of caution: Overuse can be dangerous. When you overuse this superpower, you constantly keep yourself stimulated, get overwhelmed, and feel burnt-out.

MANTRAS TO UNLOCK EMPATHY

1. Be Curious: Talk to people. Ask questions, especially to those who are different than you. Rule of thumb: When you don't know it yourself, ask. Ask how they are feeling or what they are feeling. Listen carefully when you are conversing with them. Pay attention to the non-verbal cues, expressions, gestures, etc. Follow this with the people you interact with regularly.
2. Practise Empathy: Don't just put your feet in others' shoes. Walk a mile in those shoes. If a person's behaviour bothers you, think about why it disturbs you. Instead of giving them unhelpful advice, make an effort to look past your perception of their life and choices. Consider what it's like to live their life. What are their pain points?
3. Identify Your Biases: Making assumptions, stereotyping, and being biased towards people is easy, as our brains are wired to do this. Make conscious effort to appreciate and comprehend the individuality and uniqueness of the people around you. Understand the differences while focusing on the similarities. These parallels will help you identify your bias and take control of your reactions.
4. Share Your Feelings: Don't hesitate to be seen as vulnerable. Trusting people to show your weak side builds trust and empathy.
5. Reflect and Meditate: This creates a higher level of self-awareness—of thoughts, emotions, and suffering. As a result, we move closer to understanding others' sufferings, thoughts, feelings, and actions.

In this world full of disagreements and conflicts, practising empathy is considered progress. It is an active declaration of what you stand for and a visible testament to the world you want to live in.

SUPERPOWER

9

KINDNESS

Are You God's Spouse?

'The simplest acts of kindness are by far more powerful than a thousand heads bowing in prayer.'

—Mahatma Gandhi

A little boy was standing by the stove at a tea and snacks corner. He was shivering in the cold as he was barely wearing enough clothes. Without blinking, he set his eyes on the display of the stall.

A lady watching this boy asked, 'My child, it's freezing here, and you are not even covered well.' She continued, 'What are you thinking?

'I was praying to God for me two delicious Samosas,' he replied.

The kind lady held his hand, took him inside the stall, and ordered him two samosas along with a glass of warm milk. Then she took him to the washroom to wash his hands. Taking some warm water, she gently cleaned his hands and face. She used a napkin from her bag to dry him. The child was so surprised and excited by this new experience that he started jumping on the cushioned seats. He chased the rays of flickering lights that were dancing on the floor.

Soon, their order of two samosas and a glass of warm milk arrived. The boy's mouth started watering, but he held himself back and looked at the lady.

'Go ahead, my boy,' the lady said.

The boy held the glass of milk in his small hands and finished it in no time. He then grabbed the samosa and started eating it. But he realised that the lady wasn't eating. He extended his hand to offer his half-eaten samosa.

The kind lady nodded her head, and said, 'I am full.'

Once he was finished, the lady patted his head, draped her shawl around him, and asked him to go home. The boy gave her a tight hug and ran towards his home. As the lady watched him go, he ran back to her and posed his innocent question, 'Are you God's wife?'

Self-Reflection

Settle down, sit, and relax. Close your eyes, take a few deep breaths, and let your breath become normal. Now, bring to mind the friend who is suffering, according to you, because of faults of their own. What was your response? What did you say? What was your tone? Concentrate on the physicality of gestures with them. Did you make any physical contact with them—holding hands, hugging, wiping tears? Relax and write down what you have discovered in your Evolve Journal.

Repeat this reflection exercise first by focusing your mind on a stranger when they are suffering, and then by turning your mind on your own suffering. Don't forget to take notes after each reflection.

Kindness is a Trident

Sadaa came to me seeking counselling for her son who was distant and rebellious. However, during our initial sessions, Sadaa told me a story that made me realise the issue was not with her son, but with her.

Sadaa recounted how, around five years ago, she had to leave her family for a week due to pressure from friends. Before leaving, she cooked for the entire week, filled the water bottles, and marked the clothes and food day-wise.

Although I initially thought this was a need for control, I soon realised that Sadaa was a typical Indian housewife who prioritised her family's needs above her own. She neglected herself all this time and felt guilty when she went on vacation with her friends. In her mind, being a wife and a mother was a full-time job, and any mistake on her part was a failure in meeting her duties.

Sadaa's perfectionism was causing issues in her relationship with her son. I encouraged her to practise self-compassion and let go of her need for perfection. I also suggested she take a few minutes each day to do something that brought her joy. Though she was sceptical, Sadaa revived her hobby of dancing. We helped her reframe her thoughts when she was being hard on herself.

Over time, Sadaa became more relaxed and began to let go of her need for perfection. She learnt to be kinder to herself, realising that it was okay to make mistakes and that she was doing her best. By taking care of herself, Sadaa became a better caregiver for her family. Her relationship with her son improved, and they started having real conversations with each other. Sadaa felt more secure and confident in herself, and she was no longer clueless about her son's plans, as he shared almost everything with her. Furthermore, Sadaa became a new, confident, version of herself.

The dictionary defines kindness as 'the quality of being friendly, generous, and considerate.' The word 'and' in the definition is of great importance, as it means you can be kind only when you possess the trident—the three qualities—you are friendly, generous, and considerate. It also means that not everyone friendly is kind. Similarly, a generous and considerate person can also be unkind.

Kindness is a constant choice between anger, apathy, and indifference. Being kind means you are sympathetic, large-hearted, and responsive. It means you are choosing to be good to people around you. Moreover, kindness also relates to the self, but this is where most people fail. Remember, showing kindness to others is a superpower and showing kindness to self is a 2x superpower.

Being kind is a character trait that can reduce stress and make you feel happier (Swami 2019). When we practise kindness, the body's ability to produce feel-good hormones like oxytocin, serotonin, endorphins, and dopamine improves. This makes us feel happy and in control.

Mantras to Unlock Kindness

1. Be Kind to Others: Expressing kindness is easy. You do not need to do anything big or life-changing, as a small act of kindness can also have the most impact on an individual. A genuine smile, a simple 'hello', a heartfelt 'I love you,' and a word of encouragement are more than enough.
2. Keep Your Eyes Open: Notice when others are suffering. We often fail to be kind when we fail to notice. Open the door

for strangers, help an elderly or incapacitated individual cross the road, and give a genuine compliment. Tell your loved ones how special they are. Stay away from gossip. Share your food with others. Try these simple things and notice how they make others happy.

3. Celebrate Others' Success: Be happy for others. When we ignore or minimise anyone's success, we disrespect their struggles and efforts, which makes us unkind. It is also hurtful when we bring our problems into the foreground.
4. Be Honest: Be gentle while telling the truth. Develop the courage to receive and give honest feedback.
5. Be Kind to Yourself: Self-care and self-love are not just ideas, they are vital for your continued kindness to others. When you are not kind to yourself, you often go overboard and reach your breaking point. Neglecting the self is seen in stay-at-home mothers, as they become so invested in caring for their family that they start ignoring their wants and needs.
6. 'Me' Time: Spend time with yourself and be aware of your emotions. It is important to not only recognise but also acknowledge and respect your emotions, feelings, and physical signals.
7. Avoid Comparison: No one's life is like yours just like how your life cannot be like anybody else's. So, don't compare it with others. Don't fall for the fear of missing out (FOMO).
8. Allow Slip-Ups: You can also make mistakes. You can also fail. Make sure to not set too high a standard for yourself. Don't be harsh with yourself when you fail or make mistakes.

9. Rest and Recharge: Take good rest and recharge yourself for the next mission. All acts of kindness are a mission. When you take care of yourself, you are not being selfish. On the contrary, you are being friendly, generous, and considerate to yourself.

Kindness is a gift. Gift it to yourself as well as to others.

SUPERPOWER
10

FORGIVENESS

Do You Give What You Yearn For?

'To forgive is to set a prisoner free and discover that the prisoner was you.'

—Lewis B. Smedes

Anthony Ray Hinton, an American activist, writer, and author, was wrongly convicted of two murders. He was sentenced to death and spent 28 years in prison and was on the state's death row before being exonerated in 2015. He is now cited as a classic case of racial profiling and discrimination in the United States.

After his release, he published his memoir, *The Sun Does Shine: How I Found Life and Freedom on Death Row*, in 2018. It received positive reviews, and Tim Aldama of *The Guardian* described Hinton's memoir as a story of forgiveness and struggle.'

Since then, he has been hosting book talks and readings around the country where he shares his experiences in prison. He speaks about the justice of the Alabama judicial system and other issues related to his conviction and imprisonment.

After his release, in an interview, he said, 'One does not know the value of freedom until one has it taken away. People run out of the rain. I run into the rain . . . I am grateful for every drop. Just to feel it on my face.'

In another interview, he was asked if he was angry at the people who put him in jail.

He replied, 'I forgave them all.'

The interviewer pushed, 'But they took 30 years of your life. How can you not be angry?'

Hinton responded, 'If I stay angry and become unforgiving, they will have taken the rest of my life.'

He was also quoted in another interview saying, 'The world didn't give you your joy, and the world can't take it away. You can let people come into your life and destroy it, but I refuse to let anyone take my joy. I wake up in the morning and don't need anyone to make me laugh. I'm going to laugh on my own because I am blessed to see another day. When you're blessed to see another day, that should automatically give you joy.'

Self-Reflection

Reflect on your past. Do you remember the people who have harmed you or hurt you in any way? Were you able to forgive them? Did you intentionally or unintentionally harm anyone in your life? Did they forgive you? Do you wish they had forgiven you? Pen down your thoughts in the Evolve Journal.

Forgiveness Is a Gift

Forgiveness is a word that we hate and love at the same time. We usually relate forgiveness to God, and we love the fact that

God will forgive the sinner upon confession. Yet, we despise forgiving those who have hurt us.

Who has not been hurt by the words or actions of others? Everyone has done some harm to somebody and has experienced being wronged by somebody. It could be a partner, a friend, a colleague, a neighbour, an acquaintance, or possibly a stranger. When you are hurt, you either have a choice to hold on to the bitterness and thoughts of revenge, or you can embrace forgiveness and move forward.

Menaka, a successful businesswoman, had achieved a lot in her professional life. However, despite her success, she struggled with trust issues in her intimate relationship with her boyfriend, Sameer. She came to me seeking help in building trust in their relationship. She said, 'We are deeply in love, yet I cannot fully trust him.'

Through our conversations, Menaka shared that she had been deeply hurt by someone in the past, which had caused her immense pain. She was aware that the reason behind her lack of trust was the heavy burden of heartbreak she carried. Despite trying to move on, Menaka could not let go and forgive, and this was affecting her relationships, work, and mental health.

As a coach, I helped Menaka identify and understand the impact that holding onto anger and resentment had on her life. We worked together to explore the root of her pain and the reasons forgiveness was important for her own well-being. We started by practising forgiveness through mindfulness, self-compassion, and positive self-talk. I helped her reframe her thoughts and gently nudged her to focus on the present moment rather than dwelling on the past. It was challenging, but Menaka was committed to making progress.

As our coaching sessions progressed, she successfully let go of her anger and resentment, feeling freer, happier, and more at peace than she had in years. In the end, Menaka was able to move forward in her personal and professional life with a renewed sense of purpose and confidence. She built trust in her relationship with Sameer—they got married and last year welcomed a beautiful daughter.

Forgiveness is difficult, but it is essential for healthy relationships. People cannot live together until they forgive and accept each other for who they are. Hanging on to the negative feelings can harm one's health and overall well-being. When you choose to forgive, you free yourself from past actions.

Forgiveness is a decision to let go of anger and thoughts of revenge. However, forgiving doesn't mean forgetting (Young 2007). When you forgive, you do not necessarily forget the damage. It also doesn't mean you have to be friends with the person who caused you pain. Forgiveness comes from understanding and feeling empathy and compassion for others. Forgiveness brings peace.

Mantras to Unlock Forgiveness

1. Understand the Why: Forgiving doesn't mean tolerating the terrible things that took place. It also doesn't mean the other person is innocent. It is about making a conscious choice to liberate yourself from the burden, pain, and stress that reappears when you hold on to resentment.
2. Prepare Yourself: Start with small but conscious steps towards forgiving someone (or yourself). This will ensure mental preparation.

3. Don't Argue: Avoid getting irritated at the smallest of things, such as honking when a vehicle cuts you off in traffic. Smile at the agitated people around you. Commit to not harming the offender—emotionally or verbally. Do not talk ill about others.
4. Recall: The aim here is to think about the situation objectively and to not think about the person. Ask yourself:
    a. What actions or situations do you need to forgive in a relationship?
    b. What can happen if the situation continues as it is?
    c. What change do you foresee after addressing this situation?
5. Name it to Tame It: Share your story, emotions, and pain with someone you trust. Name the offence, people, and emotions as precisely and objectively as possible. Describe why you think they would have done this and the effect of their actions on you. Lastly, share the emotions that recalling that situation triggers?
6. Take Perspective: Looking at things from others' vantage point will help you better understand their unkind words or actions. Try to:
    a. Look closely to understand where the offenders came from.
    b. What do you know about them and their circumstances?
    c. If you do not understand their 'why', can you entrust them to a superpower?
7. Confront: It is easier to forgive when the person who caused you pain is apologetic, as it means they realised their fault. Surprisingly, it does not become difficult when

they do not accept or acknowledge their fault because now you have a much better understanding of them.

   a. Do you wish to confront the person who harmed you?
   b. How do you think they would react?

8. Forgive Yourself: To err is human. We are humans and are bound to stumble and make mistakes. The trick is to not dwell on the past. Instead, make an honest confession, acknowledge your fault, and resolve to improve.
9. Commitment: Pledge to forgive by writing in your Evolve Journal or by writing a letter addressing the person who hurt you. Kindly note, you are not meant to post the letter or share the journal with the offender.

Forgiving is a process. It requires time, determination, and patience. Letting go and being forgiving is a way to peace and happiness, as forgiveness can lead to healthier relationships, better mental health, a stronger immune system, improved heart health, and a boosted self-esteem. When we choose to forgive, we lower our anxiety and stress levels, blood pressure, and experience fewer episodes of depression and hostility.

Strive to give what you yearn for—forgiveness.

SUPERPOWER 11

LOVE

Let the Beauty of What You Love Be What You Do

'Love and compassion are necessities, not luxuries. Without them, humanity cannot survive.'

—Dalai Lama XIV

A rags-to-riches success story was washing his newly purchased Mercedes with his five-year-old daughter. He lost his temper when he saw his daughter scratching the car with a sharp stone. He started hitting his child's hand without realising he had a spanner in his hand.

The girl immediately fainted from shock. She was taken to the emergency room and, on account of multiple fractures and tissue damage, she lost her fingers.

When she woke up during post-operative care, she groggily asked her mother, 'Mom, do you have some money?'

'Yes, but for what?' asked her mother.

'Dad is upset, isn't he? It's a surprise for him. Promise me you won't tell him?' She continued, 'We will go directly to the market from here to get dad's car painted, and I will buy new fingers for myself.'

The man listening to this conversation from the corner of the door was embarrassed and sorry. He went back, kicked the car, and looked at the scratch closely.

It read, 'I love you, Dad.'

Self-Reflection

Ask yourself, who do you love more—people or possessions? What do you love—the person or their qualities? Is love proportional to beauty? Can you love someone without the qualities you appreciate? Do you love people who are not related to you, your family, and your friends? Define love. Write your reflections in the Evolve Journal.

How to Show Love?

As humans, we all seek love, want love, give love, and take love. Somehow, we still can't agree on the definition of love. Some say love is deep affection, while others say it's an intense desire. For some, it is sexual passion, and for others, it is passionate affection. Some think it means devotion, and for others, it is attachment. Everyone has their own perception of love.

Rabbi Shais Taub has defined love in the best possible way: The concept of love is not a concept but an action. For me, this is the most appropriate interpretation of love, as it becomes love once it translates into action (Chapman 2010). It's the way you treat the people you love. Some claim that they love their significant others, children, parents, and friends. However, they talk to them and treat them without love. Think carefully if what you feel is actually love. Love is not only about cherishing relationships you value but also about translating your love into action, like sharing, caring, sacrificing, genuine appreciation, and much more. As it's said, our actions speak louder than words.

I once conducted a life-changing workshop titled 'Love Is an Action Verb' for the first time. The idea was to make participants aware about how they take their loved ones for granted.

We began the session with a simple discussion on how participants express love. As expected, most of them had never considered that love was more than just a feeling. They talked about the different ways in which they expressed their love, such as working hard for their families, providing financial support, and contributing in household chores.

However, it quickly became evident that while they were doing things to show their love, they were not necessarily doing them intentionally or consistently. They realised that they often took their loved ones for granted, simply assuming that their families knew they were cared for without expressing it explicitly.

To help them understand how love requires intentional effort and practise, we engaged in various activities throughout the workshop. These activities included sharing appreciation, writing down acts of kindness for loved ones, and examining beliefs and attitudes towards love.

After the workshop, participants were encouraged to continue engaging in the activities and update their progress with me on WhatsApp. Sudhanshu was the first to post his progress and a few others followed suit. Those who actively participated in these activities noticed a positive shift in their relationships, feeling more connected and experiencing improved warmth.

One participant, Sudhanshu, found the workshop particularly impactful. He approached me towards the end of the session and shared how the workshop had changed his perspective on expressing love. He recognised that he had been taking his loved ones for granted and made a promise to me that, moving forward, he will make a conscious effort to show his love through actions. The workshop had not only motivated him but also empowered him with tools and practices to make positive changes and express love in his relationships.

People display love differently—some take time and put in extra effort to truly connect with the people they love, and others easily express genuine warmth and compassion. Love has no limitations. One can love strangers, friends, family, lovers, spouse, nation, community, animals, nature, God, and the self.

Mantras to Unlock Love

1. Love Letter: Write a love letter to your loved one(s) expressing your thoughts and feelings.
2. Be an Initiator: Express your love and feelings verbally as well as non-verbally. Use physical gestures, appreciation, gifts, and surprises. Be creative!
3. Touch: Physically touch people to communicate love—holding hands, giving a pat on the back, stroking the head, sharing a hug, a kiss, or engaging in appropriate physical intimacy according to age, gender, place, time, and relationship.
4. Compliment: Give small, credible compliments to people. When you feel appreciative, say it.
5. It Starts with You: Love yourself. Take responsibility for your actions and reactions in any relationship be it personal or professional.

6. Be Curious: Talk to people, know their concerns, and understand their perspectives.
7. Be Present: Be in the moment. Meditation is a fantastic tool for this.

Do not forget love is an action verb. It involves actively doing things to show and express love, rather than just feeling it internally. Feel the love and make sure to express it, too.

SUPERPOWER 12

LISTENING

Are You Listening?

'Listening is an art that requires attention over talent, spirit over ego, others over self.'

—Dean Jackson

Shrimad Bhagavad Gita is the most remarkable example of listening. It is a compilation of 700 verses, a conversation between Arjun—a Pandava Prince—and Krishna—his charioteer.

This dialogue between the two starts on the battlefields of Kurukshetra where two massive armies—Kauravas and Pandavas—representing different ideologies face a *Dharmayuddha* (a fight against your dharma or truth) called Mahabharata. Arjun requests Krishna, the charioteer, to move his chariot to the battleground so he can see those 'eager for war'. On either side of the battlefield, he saw all his family and friends. Heartbroken, he sank into the chariot and could not hold his bow and arrows as his mind was filled with grief. For the first time in his life, Arjun was feeling helpless and was filled with melancholy, sorrow, and grief.

He expresses his pain to Krishna and shares his inner conflict. He talks about the good and evil. He speaks about how he sees no point in fighting and winning and how he won't find pleasure in this victory because it comes from killing his kin.

Throughout the entire opening chapter of the Bhagavad Gita, Arjuna speaks his mind, and Krishna listens with compassion and attention, without any prejudice.

In the following chapters, Krishna begins his discourse. He instructs Arjuna on how he should listen. He says, 'Listen with your mind absorbed in Me; it should be in love with me.'

Krishna eventually encourages Arjun to perform his duty and uphold the greater good. He shows Arjun the light in the darkness. He talks about ethical dilemmas and philosophical issues and speaks about a range of spiritual topics that go far beyond the war. Krishna displays Arjun the world after this war—victory, joy, prosperity, glory, and peace for all.

An individual's knowledge is determined by what they say, while wisdom is governed by the way they listen. peaking is the fate of knowledge, and listening is the fortune of wisdom.

Self-Reflection

Reflect on your past and observe: When was the last time you felt genuinely heard? Do you remember your feelings then? You should be able to recollect the feeling of being cared for, when you felt relaxed, calm, or open. Make note of this in your Evolve Journal.

A Powerful Way to Connect

Listening is a superpower. It is a means of gaining knowledge about things, people, events, and much more, provided one is carefully listening to others. Listening is one of the most basic and powerful ways to connect with someone. When we give our undivided attention to someone, it conveys respect and recognition to their voice. It also conveys empathy and love.

Listening is both a compliment and a commitment (Davis, Fanning, and McKay 2009). It is a commitment to listen fully—not just with the body but with the mind—to showcase a genuine effort of understanding, and to listen with an open mind.

When I was promoted as Head of the Department in my college, I was thrilled about the new opportunities and challenges that lay ahead. However, I soon realised that not everyone shared my enthusiasm. Some of my colleagues seemed distant and less willing to work with me than before.

Frustrated, I turned to my principal for advice. He was an excellent listener, and he took the time to hear me out. When I finished speaking, he encouraged me to engage with my colleagues and try to win back their confidence by taking their perspectives into account.

At first, I was hesitant to reach out, but the principal urged me to take the first step. So, I set aside some time to sit down with each of them individually. I approached each conversation with an open mind and heart, prepared to listen carefully to their concerns.

During these conversations, I paid close attention to what they were saying. I acknowledged their insecurities and showed my willingness to work with them to find solutions. By taking the time to listen, I gained a better understanding of their perspectives and was able to address some of their concerns.

This aided in building trust and strengthening our relationship. Soon enough, my team started to come around, and we worked together more efficiently and effectively than ever before. My principal's advice was priceless. He taught me that good listening skills are not only important for personal relationships but also for professional success. As a leader, it is essential to make a commitment to listening to others, even when it's difficult. This shows that you value and respect their opinions. By being a good listener, I was able to create a positive and inclusive work environment for everyone.

Listening is not just about hearing the words but peeking inside the speaker's mind. This superpower is also a skill that demands to be developed over time. Genuine listening has become rare and complicated these days. We are constantly distracted and interrupted by many things, thoughts, and people around us. While listening, we are physically there but mentally busy—agreeing or disagreeing, judging, preparing to answer, and sometimes not even thinking about this person or conversation. At times, we get impatient and keep interrupting the speaker. Sometimes, we give our opinion without even comprehending what was being said.

If we listen at all, we often listen only to the spoken words, ignoring the expressions, body language, emotions, state of mind, etc. These are the people who matter in our lives, these are our colleagues, friends, family, or neighbours. Most relationship problems these days occur because one or both parties fail to listen and instead focus on voicing their opinions. In this high-tech, high-speed, high-stressed world, personal and professional success exceedingly depends on listening and communicating.

Mantras to Unlock Listening

1. Listen Actively: You cannot listen in a passive manner. Furthermore, you must not multitask while listening. Be there, stay focused, and apply the skill of listening. The four primary goals of listening are understanding, learning, enjoying the conversation, and helping. Practise listening to refine your skills, ask questions, and give feedback.
2. Paraphrasing: Reword the conversation to communicate what you have understood. This will motivate the speaker to express freely.
3. Talk with Kindness: Put yourself in their shoes. Think through to understand where they are coming from. Give them the benefit of doubt. Don't judge, don't approach with prejudice, and don't ignore body language and emotions.
4. Keep an Open mind: Listen with kindness and give yourself time to reflect. Approach with an intention to understand the speaker, and refrain from jumping to conclusions too soon. Make sure to not approach with any preconceived notions.
5. Be Present: Give your full attention to the speaker. Mentally disconnect yourself from external distractions like activities or noises, your own thoughts, feelings, and biases. Do not focus on diction, pronunciation, mannerism, or the speaker's accent. Instead, focus on the content—both verbal and non-verbal.
6. Maintain Eye contact: Face the speaker and maintain healthy eye contact. This doesn't mean one cannot be effective when talking on the phone or from a distance. To seek a better understanding of the person, if possible, get closer. Eye contact is not about staring at people—you

can always look away and come back again. Imagine if you were talking and the person listening was looking at their phone or out of the window! You definitely wouldn't feel heard. Put your phone, paper, book, or any other distraction away. Face each other and make eye contact, even if the speaker isn't doing so.

7. Listen and Visualise: We remember the pictures better, so make a mental model when listening. Think about what the person is saying. If your attention gets diverted, bring it back as soon as you realise yourself distancing from the conversation. Concentrate on the important words and phrases.
8. Only Listen: Don't prepare for what you will ask or say next. Also, do not interrupt or start giving advises on the spot. You can think and listen faster than you speak, so relax your pace when you listen. People who have a slower pace will have difficulty expressing themselves. Let them ask for advice because they may not want a solution and are only looking for an ear to listen to them and a heart to understand. Before offering advice, provide your perspective and inquire if you have any ideas to assist them.
9. Ask Questions: Ask questions to ensure understanding. Wait for the speaker to pause, then ask the question to clarify. Sometimes, in the spur of the moment, we ask questions unrelated to the conversation, making it take another direction. If this happens, it's your responsibility to get it back on track.
10. Express Your Feelings: Don't shy away from emotions while in a conversation. Smile or laugh, do whatever the conversation demands. After all, empathy is the soul of effective listening.

11. Provide Feedback: Reflect on your understanding and the speaker's feelings. Say things like, 'You must have felt special' or 'that's terrible' or even a simple nod or a well-timed 'hmm,' 'oh,' or 'okay' works wonders. Your expressions also act as feedback.
12. Summarise: Finish your conversation by summarising everything you've heard.

Listening is an art that can only be developed through repeated practise. Like every superpower, this, too, has to be honed.

SUPERPOWER 13

SILENCE

Are You Listening to Silence?

'Speak only if it improves upon the silence.'
—Mahatma Gandhi

On a cold, dark evening, four monks lit a candle and started meditating for two weeks. A few days later, the candle flickered and snuffed out at nightfall. One monk could not resist and said, 'Oh, the candle extinguished!'

The second monk said, 'We were supposed to keep quiet and meditate.'

The third monk shouted in anger, 'Why did both of you break your silence?'

The fourth one boasted, 'Hahaha! I won.'

All four monks broke their silence for different reasons. The first monk was tempted by external factors. The second was more concerned with others breaking the rules and making mistakes than focusing on the job at hand—meditation. Anger was the reason for the third one to break his silence, and the fourth monk let his ego get in the way. He won a race that was not taking place anymore.

SELF-REFLECTION

Reflect and record your reaction to the above-mentioned story of the four meditating monks. What are your reasons for not choosing silence? Do you practise silence? When did you last spend an hour in silence?

Silence Is Golden

Silence is the most disregarded skill today. Some neglect it, others reject it, some cringe at it, and others fear it. This is happening because we are unaware of the strength of this superpower. 'Silence is Golden,' is a well-known idiom. Yet, the choice of silence is tricky for us to make. We are living in a noise-filled world, with people talking all around us at the office and home, honking vehicles, ringing phones, loud television, music, loudspeakers in temples and parties, and so much more.

Silence is difficult. These never-ending noises around us are destabilising our focus and concentration everywhere. As a result, our consistent productivity—both at work and at home—is dipping and stress levels are rising. As we hardly have any moments of silence, we miss a lot of subtle but significant details. And as we overlook details, people around us say it louder, making us miss out on more details. This becomes a vicious cycle.

Therefore, it is essential to practise moments of silence. Here, when I say silence, it is not merely the silence of words, it is the silence of thoughts. Our ego is the most significant noise in our minds. We exercise silence of withdrawal and resignation when we are hurt, tired, oppressed, or defeated. Sometimes we don't speak to others to show our dissatisfaction, discontent, or disapproval. At times, silence is imposed on people as punishment to mentally weaken them.

Each of these silences is important in its own right. However, when I intended to delve into silence as a superpower, I wanted to explore the choice of silence. Silence is a choice we make to empower ourselves and evolve as better beings. You choose silence when you choose not to be a source of the noise in your mind. This silence is about incorporating some quiet moments into daily life to achieve balance and re-establish inner peace. This silence provides much-needed rest to the mind and body from pointless noises. Silence resets the brain and relieves stress.

It also gives us an opportunity for introspection and imagination, stimulating various parts of the brain and thereby improving brain health. It aids in improving memory, concentration, and awareness. Both memory and concentration positively affect our learning ability. Silence instils patience and provides us with a sense of calm. Every time we consciously practise comfortable silence, we recharge the human battery to use our abilities better. These positive changes enhance our productivity and well-being on both the personal and professional fronts.

Harshita, an executive in a leading marketing firm, was struggling with her focus and concentration. The pressure of handling multiple tasks simultaneously had left her mind in chaos, which affected her productivity. Despite attempting multiple relaxation techniques, we couldn't find Harshita a solution because of her distractions. That's when I suggested she attend a retreat to learn meditation, and to my delight, she made the bold choice to attend a Vipassana meditation retreat.

The retreat, which required attendees to observe complete silence for ten days with no media, books, or writing materials, was held at a peaceful location nestled amidst nature. While adjusting to silence and long hours of meditation was difficult for Harshita, she pushed through the discomfort and eventually embraced the quietude.

'Sitting still in silence was the most challenging part, but in the end, there was a sense of peace and tranquillity. My mind was calm, and I had clarity that I had never experienced before. Today, even after a month, I can sit through meditation without getting distracted and concentrate on whatever I want,' Harshita recalls.

The retreat helped Harshita realise that, sometimes, tuning out external noise and distractions is necessary to hear the voice within. When she returned to work, Harshita felt a new level of self-awareness, and she noticed a difference in her ability to focus on her tasks. She became more productive and efficient, completing her work in a much shorter time.

The experience at the Vipassana retreat transformed Harshita's life, and she still practises meditation regularly, years later. She learnt that embracing silence was not about suppressing her thoughts or emotions but about learning to listen to them without judgment, both within herself and others.

Finding moments of silence is demanding and embracing silence is harder. But silence is a conscious choice we make every single day. If we embrace silence, just like Harshita, we can also avail its physical and mental benefits.

Mantras to Unlock Silences

1. Stop Talking: Silence is an uncomfortable feeling for beginners. Sometimes, we talk for the sake of talking. To get acquainted with silence, unnecessary talking must be avoided. Get comfortable with silence.
2. Disconnect with Noise: How many times do you keep your TV on without watching anything? Switch off all the devices and sit quietly. Leave your phone at home and go for a walk.
3. Practise Listening: The word 'listen' is spelled with the same letters as the word silent. Learn and practise listening to people not only with your ears but also with your heart and mind. Strive to listen to the faintest sounds, the sounds you tend to ignore—birds humming, water flowing, wind blowing, and rain falling.
4. Eat in Silence: Eat at least one meal in complete silence. No talking, no reading, no Netflix or YouTube . . . just eating.
5. Be Economical with Words: Speak only when it is better than silence. Talk with a purpose to inspire, to make others laugh, and to shower love. Choose your words wisely so that they don't hurt anyone.
6. Don't React: In a conflict, stay quiet, reflect, and respond only if needed. Don't hastily react, as it will save your energy, time, relationships, and mental peace.
7. Go Outdoors and Exercise: Currently our minds are so occupied with things that we seldom take a walk or exercise wholeheartedly. Make sure to unplug while exercising and be present. Be intentional about your body movements and the sounds of your surroundings.

8. Schedule Silence: Schedule at least two silence breaks in a day. Start with small 15-minute slots, and extend the duration when you are comfortable with appreciating silence. Once comfortable, practise it for an hour, then 12 hours, and finally stay silent for an entire day. Silence is challenging for a longer duration, but the rewards are incredible.
9. Listen to Your Silence: Focus on your silence and not the sounds around you. Silence becomes more apparent when you practise listening to it. Breathe in and breathe out. Listen to your inner voice, your heart, and your spirit.
10. Concentrate on Breathing: Silence is more accessible when the mind is engaged. Concentrate on your breathing. Breathe in and out.
11. Meditate: The mind is like an active monkey, it keeps jumping around. Practise meditation to get hold of this monkey.

Silence is golden. It's not about being quiet, rather it is about soothing the mind and relaxing the soul. Start now.

SUPERPOWER 14

TEAMWORK

How Do We Season Our Stone Soup?

'None of us is as smart as all of us.'

—Ken Blanchard

Once upon a time, there was a nomadic traveller who would travel to new destinations and stay and eat with the locals before continuing his journey. He met different people, explored himself in these uncertainties, and came across new things that were now routine to him. All this enriched his wisdom and experiences of life.

One day, during his travels, he reached a small village, and as per his usual practice, he went straight to the village sarpanch to meet the locals and find a place to stay and eat. He started talking to a group of villagers, and said, 'I am Ghanshyam, a nomadic traveller, and I am looking for a place to stay and eat for a few days.'

The simple villager replied, 'You are most welcome. We will happily offer you a place to stay, but our village has seen a drought and flood in the past few years. So, we do not have extra food. It is difficult to feed our families as is.'

The traveller said, 'Thank you for offering me a place to stay, and please don't bother with my food. I will manage that myself. In fact, I was wondering if you all would like to share my stone soup.'

'Stone soup? What's that? I have never heard of anything like this. How do you cook it?' villagers asked, amazed.

'Oh yes, stone soup! It's a miracle. I had also never heard of it until I tasted it for the first time. It is the best thing I have ever had. That's when I learnt to cook it,' said the traveller. 'If you can get me a large pot, some firewood, and water, I can make it for all of us,' he added.

The villagers rushed home and returned quickly with a pot, wood, and water. They were eager to witness the miracle. The traveller was clever, and he started the process like a ceremony. He placed the wood carefully, muttered a small prayer before setting the fire, then carefully placed the pot of water over the fire. When the water started boiling, he took out a velvet pouch from his bag and pulled out a smooth, glossy round stone. He dropped this stone carefully into the boiling water and started stirring. As he was stirring the soup, he started talking to the villagers about the soup—its taste, benefits, ingredients, and other things. He stopped talking to check his soup. He first smelt it to check the aroma, then he tasted it, exclaiming, 'Wow, this is good, but once I had stone soup with spinach. That taste was divine.'

One villager jumped from his seat and left immediately saying, 'Wait, I will get the spinach. I have some at home.'

The traveller continued, 'Oh, the soup had a base of spinach, lightly topped with finely chopped seasonal veggies and flavoured with a pinch of salt, pepper, and sugar.'

A bunch of villagers started volunteering, 'I have potatoes,' 'I will get carrots from my farm,' and 'I will get salt, pepper, and sugar.'

One villager even queried, 'Wouldn't it be better if we add some egg and pieces of meat to it?'

The traveller replied, 'It would taste heavenly! But I am not sure if all of us are okay with meat, so let's keep it simple.'

Everyone was running around fetching the ingredients. The wise traveller's job was done before the villagers could realise the pot was filled to the brim with vegetables and choices of spices. The soup was more than enough for the entire village. It was done to perfection before the traveller served the villagers bowls of this healthy, sumptuous meal.

The village sarpanch then called the traveller aside and asked him to sell the stone to him. The traveller denied for two reasons.

He said, 'I cannot give this to you. I will need it to make stone soup in the next village I stop at, and now when you know that your village has all the resources, why do you need the stone?'

He further advised, 'It is your responsibility as the head of the village to get the villagers and resources together to make the soup without the stone. Get them together because only then can everyone achieve more.'

Self-Reflection

Think about how you behave in a team. Reflect on your ability to be a team player. Explore how you can use your strengths for everything like work, partners, family, friends, relatives, etc. Note your answers in the Evolve Journal.

Teamwork Is beyond Just Your Workplace

Sukesh, an entrepreneur in the furniture manufacturing industry, had hired my organisation. He was expecting a huge surge in demand for his new line of designer furniture that they were preparing to launch. However, the company was struggling to streamline its production process, with missed deadlines and execution issues. Sukesh believed the problem lay with his team, but despite previous team-building workshops, the issue persisted.

To get to the root of the problem, our team conducted an audit, which involved meetings with various departments, visiting the production facility, and interviewing staff. We were surprised to discover that the teams that worked well individually did poorly when it came to inter-departmental collaboration. The disconnect between the sales, production, and finance teams was evident, as each department was blaming others for the cancelled orders or missed deadlines.

'It was so difficult to crack that deal,' 'You never consulted before making a tall promise of expedited delivery,' 'We cannot allow customised production without an advance,' the inter-departmental meeting looked like a fish market. We also sensed a lack of communication and empathy from top management, who were too preoccupied with routine activities to engage with their employees.

We recommended developing standard operating procedures (SOPs) and key responsibility areas (KRAs) to align departmental goals, as well as encouraging department heads to engage with their teams and with other departments. We suggested activities such as health check-ups and competitions to increase employee engagement. Finally, we proposed that department heads have lunch together as often as possible to build relationships.

Sukesh was impressed with our observations and immediately implemented our recommendations to overcome the production challenges. In less than a month's time, he noticed improved communication and collaboration among departments, better productivity, and positive results of employee engagement and satisfaction.

Sukesh's company has undergone a remarkable transformation since then. Four years have passed, and they still organise annual talent shows and regular health check-ups for their employees. They have also obtained an ISO certification, and the company is now a leader in its field, with unmatched quality and reliability.

Through this experience, we learnt that teamwork was not just limited to individual teams. Teams work best when they are engaged and when their leaders communicate to show they care. It is one of the most desirable superpowers as it provides the ability to acknowledge people's unique skills and strengths. When we talk about teamwork, it is not limited to work. A marriage is a team. Family and friend groups are teams. In fact, teamwork goes even further—good neighbourhood, city, town, and citizens. You are always a part of some team or another. In a nutshell, teamwork is a sense of social responsibility towards any group.

A team player is the one who works well within the team and are loyal and committed to the good of the group. They are reliable, do their share of work, and are willing to put the team's needs ahead of their personal ones.

However, this superpower does not come naturally to everyone. But anyone can develop it. If you feel that teamwork is vital to you in any dimension—be it career, home, society, or nation—and you wish to improve your superpower to work well in teams, make use of the mantras.

Mantras to Unlock Teamwork

1. Communicate, Communicate, Communicate: Communication is the anchor for any relationship. Work on your communication with others to develop teamwork. Make extra efforts to connect with other members of your team. Communication does not mean only 'talking', as listening to others, speaking when necessary, and engaging in timely dialogue also create effective communication. Go on a date with your partner, play with your children, plan a trip with friends, and attend at least one social gathering or activity every month to build teamwork.
2. Play Sports: Allow the spirit of friendly competition to bring your teams closer to each other. Play games like football, cricket, badminton, or any other team-based sports activity.
3. Sharing Is Caring: Share your belongings with others. Consider them as resources to be shared more than just your possessions. For instance, share clothes with friends, carpool to the workplace, offer a lift to someone on the way, or accommodate an extra person in your vehicle.
4. Don't Just Complain: Don't be an eternal pessimist. Complaining changes nothing. If you want to see a change, help others in making certain changes by making them realise what's wrong, and do what is in your power to help.
5. Focus on the Result: Teams that do not fight for credit achieve better results. Your child getting a good upbringing is the goal, so, don't bother with who is getting more credits—you or your partner. A perfectly baked cake is a

win. Even a pinch of baking powder has played its role in making it perfect. When the team wins, everyone wins. Celebrate that.

6. Show Your Passion: Don't hesitate to show your excitement. You are passionate and excited about your idea, so make sure to express it as well. Your passion, excitement, and enthusiasm will get others moving, too.
7. Manage Your Time: Develop time management skills because how you use the time available determines how well you perform in your team.
8. Align Your Goal: Strive to see the bigger picture. Align your goal with the team's goal. Recognise how you can contribute to the bigger picture and what value you receive, which will lead you to your personal goal.
9. Embrace the Difference: Differences are the soul of a team. Learn to be open to them. The differences of opinion, ability, working style, intelligence, etc., make for a wholesome working experience.
10. Lose Control: Do not make unsuccessful efforts to manage everything. Trust others and let them do their thing. Don't micromanage your team.
11. Give and Receive Feedback: Feedback can let teams grow when taken and given honestly. Learn to give and receive feedback graciously and timely. This will make the team more productive.
12. Celebrate Small Wins: Don't wait to win the war. Celebrate the small battles you win along the way.

There is no one-size-fits-all method to improve your teamwork. Experiment with these mantras and focus on your learning style, and observe what suits you. This superpower will not develop overnight. Practise humility and be supportive and open-minded to swiftly develop it.

SUPERPOWER 15

LEADERSHIP

Are You Their Leader?

'Be the change you wish to see in the world.'
—Mahatma Gandhi

The strongest display of leadership influence can be seen in the battle of Mahabharata. In the Mahabharata, when Arjuna and Duryodhana went to Krishna to ask for his support, Krishna gave them two choices—they could either have him, who would remain unarmed, or his Narayani Sena (his battalion) that was invincible. Arjun was the first to choose, and he chose the unarmed Krishna. Duryodhana was glad and filled with confidence, thinking he had a huge army on his side.

Arjuna chose unarmed Krishna over the army because he knew Krishna had the power of strategy. An army without its leader would be like an explorer without a compass—ineffective and inefficient. This choice changed the fate of the battle of Mahabharata, as Krishna helped the Pandavas level the ground, leading to their victory.

SELF-REFLECTION

Reflect on your past and answer whether you were able to decide when to follow and when to lead. Concentrate on the specific events at work or otherwise. Also focus on the way you express leadership. Make a note in your Evolve Journal.

Leadership Is Learnt

Leadership is the superpower to organise and encourage groups of people to get things done. It involves inspiring and motivating people towards a common goal. Setting goals and realising them is an integral part of leadership. To be an effective leader, one requires emotional intelligence to connect with and maintain interpersonal relationships. Good leaders handle conflicts effectively and reduce friction. They go beyond just looking at the bigger picture by providing empowering and inspiring vision.

Atul, an attendee of our Sales in Action training, had an issue with a high turnover rate in his sales team. He believed that they lacked passion and professionalism.

He said, 'No one wants to do sales. They are not committed to their work. They just don't take it seriously.'

During the team games, Atul appeared to me to be a hard taskmaster. When we probed deeper, Atul realised he had a weak connection with his team members on a personal level. As he learnt more about emotional intelligence, he began to shift his perspective and acknowledged that his cold and unapproachable personality made it difficult for his team members to share their ideas or concerns with him.

Atul was overwhelmed and wanted to change. He started engaging with the team outside of work and made conscious efforts to talk to them by cracking jokes to lighten the mood and listening to their concerns. Most remarkable change was that he tried to take their perspective and empathise with their challenges.

As Atul connected with his team members on a personal level, he saw their dedication and commitment to the job. He recognised that his team had been struggling with the high-pressure environment he had created, and by being more understanding and supportive, he could help them succeed.

Now, seven years later, Atul is a successful leader and trainer. He opens each one of his leadership training sessions with the powerful realisation he had during our Sales in Action training programme: 'Managers focus on changing others to get the job done, but leaders turn to themselves and make it happen.'

Leadership is about leading all sorts of people; thus, good leaders must reflect diversity. However, there is no set formula for good leadership skills as all trailblazers approach leadership differently, possessing distinct styles. Your leadership style can look very different from that of your friend's or colleague's. One can be a quiet and soft leader, and the other a bold and extroverted one—both can be successful. We cannot pinpoint specific personality traits that best contribute to good leadership. That's good news because it means you can develop this superpower around your natural strengths.

Forming the superpower of leadership can transform your life, because communication and emotional intelligence are integral parts of leadership. They can empower your career and your private life as they enhance your relationship with people. In the process of harnessing your natural skill set, becoming more self-aware and in-tune with strengths and weaknesses, empowers you as a person.

No one is born a leader. Most people have some natural superpowers, but being aware of them and capitalising on them can change the game.

Mantras to Unlock Leadership

1. Organise Events: Take initiative in organising and leading an event or activity at work or in your family. For instance, organise a family event including all generations, bringing all the age groups together, or throwing a birthday party at work.
2. Build Encouragement: Encourage people from different generations to speak, as everyone's perceptions are important. Involve everyone, even the ones who talk less or the ones who feel left out in conversations. Assign them a task—or a goal—to be completed.
3. Stand Up: Speak up if anyone is being bullied, harassed, or treated unfairly. Encourage fairness on both personal and professional fronts.
4. Be a Role model: You can inspire people only when you practice what you preach. A leader knows the way, shows the way, and goes the way. Therefore, lead by example and show them what you expect from them.
5. Connect with People: Communicate with people to know them, to win their trust, and to build rapport. Invest in people and relationships as it is a vital aspect of leadership.
6. Be Curious: Ask questions, read, conduct research to be better equipped with information, ideas, and the wisdom of good leadership. An I-know-it-all mindset can hinder growth, so be curious and open to learning more.

7. Help Others: Extend a helping hand to people, friends, family, colleagues, or anyone in need. Assist them in learning new skills and help them grow.
8. Perspective-Taking: Not being able to take perspective is the deadliest enemy of a leader. Learn to adopt different viewpoints.
9. Give Credit: Give due credit to your team members promptly. This will not only encourage those who are self-motivated and contribute daily but also inspire everyone else to work to their fullest potential. Doing so can make you a strong leader with an even stronger team.
10. Empathy: Empathising with people can provide great perspective, as it can improve listening—a vital skill for leaders.

Investing in yourself is the mantra to reveal your full potential. Challenge yourself every day to be open and be an avid learner.

SUPERPOWER 16

FEEDBACK

Are You Ready for the Feedback?

'The key to learning is feedback. It is nearly impossible to learn anything without it.'

—Steven D. Levitt

When I worked for a business school as a professor and associate director, I categorically remember this argument with my assistant professor, Pratap, regarding course completion. I was new to this administrative role and wanted to complete the course as per the academic calendar. Pratap was young and passionate about academics and wanted to focus more on the concepts and quality of his delivery instead of the calendar.

We were arguing in front of the director, Sarita, in her office. There was a heated exchange of words when, finally, Pratap got up to leave and said, 'Whatever!'

I leaned back in my chair and looked at Sarita, thinking it went well, as if I had won a battle. I was expecting a smile, a gesture of encouragement, or a pat on my back. However, Sarita got up from her seat, sat next to me, and held my hand.

She said, 'You behaved like a bully. You cannot harass your subordinates to get things done.'

Hearing this came as a shock to me. I was of the belief that I was doing good by getting things done. I always knew I was a bit direct and overly honest at times, but was not prepared for the feedback Sarita gave me. I had been working with Sarita for five years, and she was the one who recommended me for all my promotions. She had always been nice to me, so when she said that I didn't act properly, all I heard was, 'You behaved like a bully! You harass your subordinates.'

This took a lot of time to sink in.

Self-Reflection

Did my story remind you of a similar situation you may have encountered? Did you handle it well? Reflect on that situation and note down the details in your Evolve Journal. Who gave you the feedback? What was its purpose? Was it helpful? Was it honest? Do you give feedback honestly?

Creating a Feedback Loop

Feedback is a two-way process. In fact, it is a loop. When you offer constructive feedback, people are more inclined to give you some themselves. Both giving and receiving feedback gracefully and honestly are superpowers. Whenever we respond, we give feedback—whether it is a response expressed as silence, criticism, or praise. Whatever your action or inaction is, you are giving feedback.

While receiving feedback, we often defend ourselves or make excuses, especially when it's negative. But when you are a modest individual, you would typically completely deny the positive things said about you. You might revel in the praise when what you need to do is reflect.

Both giving and receiving feedback are essential for personal growth. You need to improve upon both to be helpful. Providing feedback is about specificity—strive to give details and provide more information to the person receiving the feedback.

On the other hand, receiving feedback is probing. Ask questions and get more information from the person giving you feedback. Feedback is most helpful when it provides a detailed information about the actions of the receiver. Feedback can be labelled as 'detailed' when it passes through three simple checks:

Is the feedback specific?

Is the feedback accurate and timely?

Has enough inquiry gone into the feedback—both before and during the feedback discussion?

Pass feedback from these three checks before processing it. While feedback can take many forms, we solely focused on verbal feedback given or received immediately after the action.

Mantras to Unlock Power of Feedback

While Giving Feedback

1. Check the Readiness: Check whether the person is ready for feedback. You can even seek permission by asking: 'Hope you don't mind taking feedback?' or 'Can we debrief on this?'

2. Focus on the Act: Don't confuse action with the person. While giving feedback, avoid talking about the attitude or characteristics of the person, and speak only about the specific actions. For instance, don't call them unprofessional. Instead, point out the errors they are making—not meeting deadlines or showing up late at work.
3. Be Specific: Good feedback is specific and detailed. Start answering the '4Ws and an H' to ensure that feedback is specific and detailed. What happened? When and where did it happen? Who was involved? How does it impact others? Consider saying, 'This Biryani you made today is awesome,' instead of, 'You always cook awesome food.'
4. Be Sincere: Effective feedback should always be honest and sincere as its purpose is improvement. Your conviction reflects when you are honest in your feedback. When the feedback is negative, it reflects that you are concerned and wish to help. Superficial and artificial feedback appears like flattery, and a non-sincere one seems like an insult.
5. Be Prompt: Feedback is an ongoing process so don't make it look like an occasional thing. Don't wait for the review meetings—in a professional set-up—and do not bottle it up—on the personal front. Good feedback should be timely.
6. Stop and Listen: Feedback is not a one-way street. Let the recipient speak. Let them ask questions. Let them probe deeper. Let them justify their actions and choices. Let them give their reasons. Let them react. Stop and take time to understand their position.
7. Expect Resistance: Although no one enjoys negative feedback, some may even deny the positive ones. Let the

feedback sink in. Communicate what is expected and how it can impact them or others.

8. Withold Judgement: Instead of saying, 'You should have done that,' 'You shouldn't have said that,' simply offer your feedback on what has happened, what action was right or wrong, and why.
9. Avoid Assumption: Do not assume why the person acted the way they did and say, 'You are late because you don't respect our time.' Don't speculate at all.
10. Don't Be Harsh: Respectful and careful feedback is productive, but harsh feedback can be counterproductive. Be empathetic and respectful, as well as be cautious of the receiver's feelings, state of mind, and readiness to take the feedback.
11. Don't Provide Solutions: The aim of feedback is self-reflection. Don't give a quick-fix solution. Instead, ask them questions and make them understand what they did well, what they did wrong, why this has happened, if they need to fix it, and what they can do to fix it.

While Receiving Feedback

1. Seek Feedback: When you ask for feedback, it's no longer a surprise for you. That way you are better prepared to receive it, process it, and ready to learn and change.
2. Be Receptive: Listen, let it sink in, and then process the feedback. Don't rush to give explanations, excuses, or reasons. Control your defensiveness because this will discourage the person providing feedback. They will not offer any in the future because they don't want to hurt you or deal with your defensive behaviour. Whenever you

find yourself getting defensive, take a deep breath to gain control of yourself.

3. Listen Carefully: Practise active listening to fully understand the feedback. Pay attention to the words, pauses, silences, body language, and emotions. Encourage them to talk.
4. Reserve Opinion: Feedback is an opportunity for learning about yourself. While gauging others' viewpoints, you are also learning how your actions and reactions are interpreted by them.
5. Reflect and Probe: Pass the feedback through the first two checks:

   Is it specific?

   Is it accurate and timely?

   Have a third check and probe to get that third check right. Ask questions for clarification and better understanding. Summarise what you have understood.
6. Acknowledge the Giver: Feedback is a gift, so make sure to thank the giver for it. Acknowledge that they have taken a risk. Always start by saying thank you and acknowledge their efforts.
7. Not All Feedback Is Useful: All feedback is a perception. People often think what they already believe. Although they are watching our actions, they interpret them based on their ability. All of us are prey to biases and filters that continue to form, change, and break with experiences. Just because someone is giving feedback does not mean that the feedback is correct. It is important to pass all feedback through the above-mentioned three-step check.

8. Check Reliability: Check with others to determine the reliability of the feedback. Is it the opinion of only one person? If that's not the case, they should bother about it when they are the only ones who feel or believe it, not you.
9. Decide the Way Forward: Even good feedback is useless if it does not achieve anything other than immediate disappointment or gratification. Only you have the right and the ability to decide the way forward. What to do with the feedback is only your prerogative.
10. Wait to React: You are angry, upset, and hurt. You find the feedback highly objectionable and demeaning, and you disagree with the feedback. It's best to not react on an impulse. Wait till your emotions are under control.

Giving and receiving feedback can be uncomfortable and unpleasant for people who don't know how to express it. Improving at feedback will provide you with an accurate picture of your strengths and weaknesses. One can leverage the superpower of giving and receiving feedback by encouraging open communication and building trust thereby leading to stronger relationships.

SUPERPOWER

17

RESILIENCE

Do You Accept Your New Reality to Make Progress?

'I have not failed. I've just found 10,000 ways that won't work.'

—Thomas Edison

Once upon a time, there was a brave king who fought many battles. When defeated, he ran away from the battlefield and hid in the forest to save his life. The enemies then took over his empire.

In the forest, he saw a spider struggling to reach its web on the tree. It slipped frequently but it kept trying, and after several attempts, it reached the web. The king, who was watching the spider, noticed how, with every failed attempt, the spider could reach further than the previous one. That day, the spider taught a valuable lesson to the king. Filled with hope and courage, he started preparing for battle with his limited men. He lost the battle seven times before finally being able to win his empire back.

As per the folklore, this legendary king was Vikramaditya from the illustrious Gupta Empire (first century BCE).

Self-Reflection

Before you start, spend some time reflecting on your life. Ask yourself, 'Do I remain calm in tense circumstances?' 'Do I know how to cope with a setback?' 'How well do I handle criticism?' Make a note of your answers in your Evolve Journal.

The Importance of Resilience

Resilience is a fantastic superpower that helps us change, adapt, and recover after a setback. It is a superpower that keeps us moving despite difficult situations and undesirable results. Anyone can fail, but only a resilient individual can dream and imagine the triumph of trying again. A resilient person can boldly face challenges and failures, as they do not stop after a failure. They accept the defeat, analyse the mistakes, adapt to the change, and begin again.

A very unsettling voice answered on the other side of the call, 'Please help me, I don't want to lose her.'

Veena, a worried mother, called me seeking help for her daughter, Vaisnavi, who had been distressed since the day she received her 11th-grade exam results. Vaisnavi was getting disconnected from her world. She stopped talking, going out with friends, or engaging in her favourite hobbies like playing video games and dancing. Although Vaisnavi was a bright student, she found it difficult to concentrate in class, leading her grades to slip. Her parents had tried everything to help her, but nothing seemed to be working. They were terrified that if Vaisnavi did not improve soon, she would fail her exams and lose all hope of a successful future.

When I met Vaisnavi and her parents, I could tell that there was a disconnect between her heart and head. She had been studying science and wanted to become a doctor to make her parents proud since both of them were doctors. However, her heart was in the Humanities. To discuss the probable cause, I asked her parents to meet with me alone for the next session.

Initially, they were perplexed and said, 'We have never forced Vaisnavi to do anything!' But soon they realised that the environment in the house was affecting Vaisnavi's subconscious, and they were all in to make amends.

Over the next few weeks, we worked closely with Vaisnavi, giving her personalised attention and support.

One day, Veena called and asked, 'What magic have you done, Swati? Vaisnavi can't stop dancing today!'

This was the day when Vaisnavi realised where her heart was as we were discussing her passion—her why. When Veena and her husband, Vishal, contacted the school to request a change of subject for 12th grade, Vaisnavi was overwhelmed. She had an uphill task ahead of her—first, she had to complete the 11th-grade syllabus, and then prepare for her board exams.

We decided to take it one step at a time. I asked Vaisnavi to make a vision board. She was high on energy and made a beautiful vision board for herself that included a picture of her dream college among other things. Then she made her SMART syllabus goals. An education counsellor helped her chop the large, overwhelming goals into bite-sized milestones. Both parents helped her evaluate her progress and motivated her with the right rewards. Vaisnavi also received full support from her schoolteachers. They encouraged her to ask questions and gave her constructive feedback on her progress.

Slowly but surely, Vaisnavi showed improvement and was beaming with confidence. She became more focused in class, more engaged in her learning, and started enjoying the entire process. She was following her heart. Not only did Vaisnavi do well in her exams, but she also scored a place in her dream college, eventually graduating as a university topper. She is now pursuing her research in Sociology.

Feeling sad and fearful after a failure, rejection, loss, or trauma is natural. It is also natural to feel overwhelmed by ambiguity and turbulence. To stop and slow down after such an event is also normal. Nonetheless, resilience determines whether you start over again and how quickly you can do so after a failure. It puts a timeline on how long it will take you to start again. Resilient people accept and adapt to changes promptly. They stay calm even in stressful situations, taking care of not only themselves but also others and encouraging them to face the challenges.

Those who lack resilience focus more on the problems, feel victimised and overwhelmed, and may resort to unhealthy coping practices, such as drugs and alcohol. Resilient people consider difficult situations as challenges that need an active response. It provides them a reason to get up every morning and focus on what's in their control. Resilience is not the solution to any problem; however, it certainly is the reason for their happiness. Such individuals are optimistic and can see the light at the end of the tunnel.

Mantras to Unlock Resilience

1. Smarter Goals: Your aim should be big enough to keep you engaged and motivated so that you don't leave it midway. Goals should be small enough to keep challenging you, but not overwhelming. Your goals should be SMART—

simple, measurable, actionable, realistic, and time-bound. Once the goal is smart and you have started acting on it, evaluate the progress from time to time and reward yourself for achieving milestones. That's what I call making a goal SMARTER.

2. Stay Flexible: Be ready to change your sail when faced with unexpected winds. It's a skill to adapt to any situation and change plans.
3. Focus on Wellness: When the body and mind are healthy and relaxed, it's easier to handle stressful situations. Take care of your overall well-being. Stay conscious of the five pillars of wellness every day—eating healthy, hydrating properly, exercising regularly, sleeping soundly, and meditating daily.
4. Watch Your Inner Dialogue: Don't let negativity derail you. Practise positive thinking. When you find yourself using words like, 'always,' 'never,' 'why only me,' and/or 'I can never,' change the tone of how you speak to yourself.
5. Take Perspective: Stress skews our outlook. Investigate the situation, see all the possibilities, and find the light.
6. Exercise the Power of Choice: One can react in panic and lose forever, or one can stay calm, think, adapt, and make necessary changes. The choice is yours.
7. Evaluate Failure: Failure is an opportunity to reflect, evaluate, and make positive life changes. It can lead you closer to your goal because you are aware of what doesn't work for you. Ask yourself: 'What went wrong?' 'Is there anything I can do about it?' 'What can I do to correct it?' When you ask the right questions and find the answers, you achieve post-traumatic growth.

8. Find Your Why: People with a clear 'why' are more resilient. What is the purpose for you to start something? Once this intent is crystal clear, you develop resilience.
9. Ask for Help: When in need, say it. Build connections to confide in, share the load, and find perspectives. Develop relationships you can completely rely on. Remember, this is a two-way street. Be ready when they are in need as well.
10. Keep Learning: Honing your skills, learning new ones, and working on yourself makes you confident and resilient. Keep refining your existing strengths and building new ones.

The ultimate mantra for developing the superpower of resilience is to remember that the best is yet to come.

SUPERPOWER 18

PERSEVERANCE

Do You Finish What You Start?

'It always seems impossible until it is done.'
—Nelson Mandela

A Giraffe learns the most powerful life lesson right after its birth in a series of nerve-wracking experiences. First, the mother giraffe gives birth to her baby, which falls from the mother's womb to the ground at a height of around 8 feet. The weak calf lies still and pants after impact.

The mother lowers her neck to clean her calf and then, unexpectedly, kicks the baby with her legs to launch it in the air, causing it to fall again. After sustaining another fall, the baby lies on the ground, panting. She kicks her calf again and again. This surprising matronly behaviour continues until the baby pushes itself on its own legs and stands up.

The calf shakes and battles to find balance when the mother comes and gives it yet another kick. The baby topples once more. However, this time, it stands up quickly and starts running. As the mother giraffe taught her calf to survive, she is delighted!

Self-Reflection

Think about what you did when you failed in your attempts to achieve your goals. Have you started again? Did you reflect on your goals and abilities? Did you find a mismatch? Did you start over with any change(s)? Will a change in your abilities, effort, direction, approach, or goal help you? Write your answers in your Evolve Journal.

Finish What You Start

Perseverance is the superpower that keeps you going till you finish what you have started. It nudges you towards your goal over time, even when you face obstacles, complications, or setbacks. This superpower makes one practise for perfection, learn from failures, resist immediate gratification as well as teaches one to focus on achieving a larger goal. It also keeps one motivated and optimistic by building endurance for pain and discomfort. Perseverance determines the length and the strength of your efforts before you succeed, especially when it is not going as planned.

Arjun was our strength coaching client and was passionate about serving his country by getting a government job. He had appeared for several examinations but did not get through. Arjun, however, believed that he could make a difference in his country by serving the government but was unsure because of the negative comments from family and friends about his never-ending struggle.

We did Arjun's VIA (Value in Action Inventory) of strengths to find out what strengths were in play. Kindness, fairness, and perspective were amongst his top five strengths that perfectly aligned with his passion. On the other hand, perseverance and hope were somewhere at the bottom, which could be the reason for his failure.

Our objective was to help Arjun use his top positive strengths to his advantage. I gave him a perspective—you either win or learn. Every experience, even if it doesn't result in immediate success, is an opportunity to learn and grow.

I was able to intrigue Arjun, he started analysing his past mistakes and looking for areas that he could improve on for better performance in his next exam. Arjun's mindset had changed.

Arjun's family and friends continued to taunt him, but it didn't faze him. He knew that he was doing his best to make a positive impact, and that was all that mattered to him. He also started participating in social work activities to fuel his passion and make a difference in his community.

Eventually, Arjun's perseverance paid off. He landed a government job he had always wanted. He was thrilled to finally have the opportunity to serve his country and make a difference. Even after securing the job, Arjun didn't forget the lesson he had learnt and continued to inspire others who were struggling to achieve their dreams. Success is not just about winning, it is also about learning, growing, and moving till you reach your destination.

Perseverance is often confused with resilience. They both have common traits, however, the key difference is in what both these superpowers provide you individually. Resilience determines how long it will take you to start again after facing failures. Perseverance determines how long you can go on and how strong you come back after each failure.

Mantras to Unlock Perseverance

1. Discover Passion: It's easier said than done. To discover your passion, try various things and observe passionate people with curiosity. You might not have the same passion or goal, but that inquisitiveness can lead the way.
2. Make and Break Your Goal: Once you align your goal with your passion, break it down into smaller parts with well-defined milestones. Pick one at a time. Success is the sum total of all past wins and losses.
3. Find Your Why: When you know what your passion and purpose are, it becomes easier to see the fruits of your labour. At that point, you recognise what you will receive is worth the pain. This makes the journey exciting and enjoyable.
4. Practise: Practise makes perfect. It hones your skills, expands your strengths, and reduces your weaknesses. Focus on effort over results. Even when you miss the bull's eye, the sheer effort will get you closer to your target.
5. Review, Reflect, and Adapt: Ask for feedback on your performance from others. Conduct a self-review as well. Consider what's lacking and make changes wherever there is scope for improvement.
6. Maintain Hope: Believe that you are moving in the right direction. Know how your actions will improve your future and can make all the difference.
7. Feedback: Immediate and positive feedback can instil perseverance. You can do it with others to keep them on track. You can also ask your family, friends, or trustworthy people to be your cheerleaders and give you honest feedback.

Perseverance is your ability to balance your wants and goals amidst life's uncertainties and obstacles. This superpower improves your odds of winning.

SUPERPOWER
19

ZEST

Are You Living in a Rut?

'Everything has beauty, but not everyone sees it.'
—Confucius

A sixteen-year-old girl met with a road accident. Upon regaining consciousness, she felt a stinging pain in her legs. She could not move her body. Her legs were bleeding. All her memories started replaying in her head—her happy middle-class family, how her mother was living her dreams through her by watching her dance, her being the most promising dancer in the class. She aspired to be a dancer. She wondered, *Will I be able to dance again?*

Some passer-by took her to the hospital. A few cuts and a fractured femur bone were the extent of her injuries. A medical intern sutured her wounds and applied the cast to heal her fractured bone. Seven days later, she visited the doctor complaining of acute pain. The doctor removed the plaster and discovered she'd contracted gangrene on her leg. Amputation was the only way forward.

Her right leg was amputated, just three inches below the knee. All her dreams dimmed at that moment, and her life became difficult. Every day became a challenge as she could barely walk on one leg. After some time, she regained mobility with the help of a prosthetic leg. Then, for her, there was no looking back. She returned to dancing two years after the accident.

Furthermore, she also performed for the public on global stages. She even debuted in the movie industry with the Telugu film *Mayuri* based on her own life. Later, this film was dubbed into several other Indian languages. This film was released as *Nache Mayuri* in Hindi. This girl is none other than Sudha Chandran. She is now a famous actor and has won several awards and many hearts.

Self-Reflection

Reflect by asking yourself some tough questions. Write in your Evolve Journal. Are you living life to the fullest and making the most out of every day? Does it feel like you're stuck in a rut?

Examine the routines and activities of your day. Ask yourself which experiences bring you the most energy and enthusiasm, and if you wish to create more of these.

Live Each Day Like a Child

Zest is the enthusiasm and energy to live life every day like a child. This superpower makes life worth living. Life is not easy for any of us as we all have our own struggles and challenges to face. Some people are struggling to maintain their reputation in society, some for money, some for a position, some for a job, some for bigger goals, some for plain survival, some for meaning, and some for two square meals.

I was conducting a stress management session for a group of twenty-five young DSPs in the tranquil and picturesque surroundings of Pachmarhi. As the session progressed, I asked the participants to share the reasons that contributed to their stress.

One by one, the DSPs spoke about their long, erratic duty hours that kept them away from their families, making it difficult to maintain a healthy work-life balance. They also mentioned the absence of a fixed schedule and the stress that came with the unpredictability of their work. They spoke about the pressure to perform and the weight of responsibility that accompanied their job.

As I listened to their stories, I couldn't help but feel a sense of empathy and understanding. I wanted to help find these young DSPs a way to cope, so I introduced them to the concept of zest. I explained that zest was all about finding joy and enthusiasm in life even in the face of stress and adversity. I talked about the importance of self-care, taking time for oneself, and doing things that bring joy and meaning to life.

Initially, the participants were sceptical, thinking that focusing on zest was a luxury they couldn't afford given the demands of their job. However, Nisha, who was in charge of the training programme and was stationed at Pachmarhi, asked the participants if they had noticed the clouds, taken deep breaths in the clean air, or taken time to relax their minds in Pachmarhi's pleasant natural habitat?

Nisha's questions intrigued everyone, and as we continued talking, all the participants realised that cultivating zest was not just a nice-to-have quality but a necessary conscious choice of keeping the child inside us alive.

We set about exploring ways to cultivate zest in our lives. We made our training session a no-cell phone zone, took walks together in the beautiful surroundings of Pachmarhi, and sat in silence, appreciating the beauty of nature and the simple pleasures of life. We also discussed how cell phones can be a great way to stay in touch with our loved ones, but they also can be a cause of losing out on those special moments of life by stealing our mindfulness.

I could see a change in them instantly. They were enjoying little moments, smiling, laughing, talking, and listening like never before. They were aware that they would still face the same challenges and stresses when they returned to work, but they had discovered zest that would keep them positive and playful and help them navigate those challenges with greater ease.

Fast forward a few months, and it was an 'Aha!' moment for me when a couple from this training—Rajesh and Priya—paid me a visit and shared that they had continued to practise the principles of zest in their daily lives. Rajesh shared that since the training session, he had made it a point to go on a walk every morning, which helped clear his mind and improved focus. Priya had started journalling and found that it helped her release her thoughts and emotions. They had made changes to their routines, prioritising self-care, celebrating small wins, and connecting with their loved ones more often.

I felt a sense of fulfilment. I crossed my fingers and wished them luck as they continued to look after their well being and bring joy and enthusiasm into their lives. I thanked the divine for giving me the chance to make a difference.

Remember your days as a child. You smiled without reason. Your eyes always sparkled. Life was full of excitement and energy. You anticipated the day ahead. You were carefree and each day was a thrill.

You grew older and things changed. You turned into dull, boring adults. Now, your shoulders carry the weight of heavy bills, fees, groceries, travel, medicine, and whatnot. You are always preoccupied with commitment, duties, and responsibilities. You don't live in the moment . . . you live in the past or the future. This causes stress and anxiety, as you are either not pursuing what you love or you do not love what you pursue. In both cases, the spirit of life is lost.

Zest and happiness go hand in hand. Someone who approaches life with excitement and energy seldom does things half-heartedly. They always feel active and alive. Zest nurtures our souls and brings energy to life.

Mantras to Unlock Zest

1. Keep it Simple: Complexity and busyness are the enemies of zest. Keep your life simple, and do not plan everything; leave some space for surprises in life. Avoid stressful situations, forgive people for their mistakes, resolve friction early, live within your means, declutter, and downsize.
2. Mindful Living: When you are busy and rushing around all day, you often miss out on the special moments. This robs you of your zest. You forget to dance in the rain, bask in the sunshine, experience your child growing, and much more. Stay in the present. Don't overcommit, learn time management, and wake up early (Sharma 2018). Spend more time with nature and meditate to realise its beauty.
3. Physical Well-Being: Eat healthy, exercise regularly, sleep well, stay hydrated, and meditate. Also make sure to get regular medical check-ups.
4. Exercise: A little discomfort is good. Regular exercise and an active lifestyle increase zest in an individual.

Resistance is the way to liveliness. Do something that your body resists.

5. Take Risk: Risk invokes adventure, which, in turn, requires enthusiasm and energy. Step out of your comfort zone to do something new.
6. Have Fun: Do some activities that give you happiness every day. Rekindle your lost hobbies. Plan and do one thing you look forward to every day, and break the monotonous rut and surprise yourself.
7. Socialise: Spend time with family, friends, and loved ones. Cultivate new relationships, do random group activities, and engage in social service. Be enthusiastic about meeting and greeting other people.
8. Meditate: Spend more time with yourself and learn to sit in silence.

Resilience, perseverance, and zest are part of the same deck—happiness. Resilience determines how long you take to recover from a failure. Perseverance determines the length and force of your efforts. Zest determines how you will enjoy the journey. In failure and gain, achievements and pain, and even without a game, zest will get you there. You will also enjoy the process.

SUPERPOWER 20

HONESTY & INTEGRITY

Can the Truth Set You Free?

'I am not bound to win, but I am bound to be true. I am not bound to succeed, but I am bound to live by the light that I have.'

—Abraham Lincoln

Children lined up on the racetrack on the school's sports day. They were waiting for the race to start. Everyone started running towards the finish line immediately after hearing, 'On your marks, get set, and go.'

Raju took a leap, closely followed by Sanju. Sanju was pushing hard to beat Raju when an unexpected event occurred. Raju lost his balance and fell right in front of Sanju, causing Sanju to fall as well.

Mahesh, who was running for the third position, stopped and offered them a hand. They held hands, and all three started running together to the finish line. None of them could claim the title. All three finished the race.

Self-Reflection

Sit back, relax, reflect, and ask yourself, 'Was this the right thing to do?' 'Can Mahesh be me?' Also reflect on the 'why' aspect of your answer in your Evolve Journal.

Honesty and Integrity Are Different

Man is a social animal. We thrive on complex relationships. Of the many essential elements for a thriving relationship, trust is the most important one. This binding trust comes from honesty and integrity. These superpowers are integral to your evolution.

If Mahesh had not stopped to help his fallen opponents, he would have claimed the first position well within the rules of the game. This is honesty. However, he chose the spirit of the game over winning. That is integrity. The debate can continue because it's the individual's perspective.

During our consultancy project with Sukesh, from Chapter 14, they were under immense pressure to meet their sales targets. We recommended that his sales team undergo the Sales in Action module. The team was taking risky shortcuts and making promises they couldn't keep—a clear breach of honesty and integrity.

At first, Sukesh and his team were resistant to the idea. They believed that they needed to make tall promises to meet their targets, even if they couldn't deliver on them. However, the Sales in Action module emphasised the importance of building trust with clients to establish a long-term relationship, rather than just focusing on short-term gains.

The trainers encouraged the sales team to be assertive with their clients about what they could deliver. Initially, the sales team was reluctant when the trainers asked them to appraise and apologise to their clients whose orders were getting delayed. But the trainers showed them how they could use assertion to their benefit.

Ram was the first to step up and take action. He summoned the courage to call the first client and admit that he had underestimated the project's scope and would need more time to complete it. He apologised for his mistake and promised to make it right. To his surprise, the client was impressed with Ram's honesty and appreciated his willingness to admit his mistake. Ram's experience gave others courage, and soon, all the clients were appraised. Most clients appreciated the honesty and were happy to work with Sukesh and his team, even if it meant waiting a little longer for their orders.

The pressure was relieved, the sales team no longer had to worry about constant updates and complaints from clients, and the production team was no longer working overtime to meet unrealistic deadlines.

The impact of this new approach was immediate. With honesty and integrity at the forefront of their sales approach, Sukesh and his team not only improved their business and relationships with clients but also within the organisation.

From that day on, Sukesh and his team recognised that honesty and integrity were essential in building a successful business. They decided to make honesty and integrity a core value of their company. They haven't looked back since.

Honesty is about being true to others and speaking the truth. It is also about doing what you preach. Honesty is about being transparent without pretence and being genuine in the way we act. It is taking responsibility for one's feelings and actions. Honesty is being true to others in your words, actions, and behaviours. The focus of honesty is on others, not you.

Integrity is one notch over honesty. It is not only about being honest but also about having strong moral principles. It means one is true to others but also to themselves. Integrity means you not only preach and practice but also believe it to be true. Integrity is living life according to your morals and values. It focuses inwards on the self.

One can be honest without integrity, but one cannot have integrity without honesty. By practising the superpowers of honesty and integrity, one can avoid unnecessary personal and professional stress, anxiety, and confusion in relationships. Both these elements bring success and peace in both personal and professional lives.

Mantras to Unlock the Power of Honesty and Integrity

1. Speak the Truth: Don't avoid difficult conversations. Express yourself clearly and with honesty.
2. Think before Committing: Start small. Don't overcommit and make sure to think twice before making promises. Take small steps towards your goal.
3. Respect Boundaries/Choices/ Diversities: Love and respect others—their choices, boundaries, and diversities. Integrity is living in peace with your morals and values. Remember, that's your choice, and don't force them on others. Respect their boundaries (time, ability, finances, etc.) and choices within relationships.
4. Help People: Help others but prioritise self-care. Help yourself before helping others. Help others to empower them, not to make them dependent on you.
5. Appreciation: Genuinely compliment, appreciate, and give credit to the ones who deserve it.

6. Collaborate with Others: Collaboration—not competition—makes all the parties winners.
7. Meet Deadlines: Honesty and integrity at work start with respecting deadlines.
8. Don't Abuse Power: Your power, position, status, and intelligence are not to be abused but used in positive ways. For instance, if you work in an influential role and people offer you gifts, consider if you should accept them.
9. Be Accountable: Take responsibility for your actions in both success and failure. Whatever you say, own it and mean it.
10. Be Assertive: Saying no is an art. Learn this art. Speak and stand for yourself.

Hone this superpower of honesty and integrity for your happiness, satisfaction, success, well-being, and peace.

SUPERPOWER 21

COURAGE

How Attached Are You to Your Rope?

'I learned that courage was not the absence of fear but the triumph over it.'

—Nelson Mandela

There lived a brave man who wanted to climb a mountain's highest peak. This mountain was an everyday sight from his window. Thus, he started practising the craft of mountaineering. A few years later, he took the plunge, but others were afraid, so, he went unaccompanied.

Days and nights passed by, and he kept climbing. One fateful and cold night, darkness and strong wind made him slip and lose control. It was a free fall. He kept tumbling and falling downhill like a weightless ball. He was terrified. His life flashed before his eyes. He was reminded of all the good and evil he had done in his life.

Suddenly, these thoughts were interrupted by a hard pull of the rope tied around his waist. His fall had stopped, and he was hanging by the rope. He cried and screamed, 'Help, help, help . . .'

He heard a frail voice, 'Just do what I say.'

The man cried, 'Yes, I will. Just save me.'

The frail voice said, 'Cut the rope and free yourself.'

'Are you mad?' holding the rope with a stronger grip. He cried again, 'Help me, please.'

The frail voice said, 'Have faith and just cut the rope.'

The man could not endure cutting the rope and held on for dear life. The following day, the rescue team recovered a frozen body holding onto a frozen rope dangling six feet above the ground.

Self-Reflection

How attached are you to your rope? Will you let go? Answer these questions in your Evolve Journal. Note that you need courage to keep going, but you need greater courage to let go.

Courage is not fearlessness, nor is it the absence of fear. Courage is taking action *despite* fear. It is the willingness to respond even in the face of fear. Breaking the status quo and embracing change is the most admirable act of courage, as it often requires confronting deeply ingrained beliefs and systems that have been in place for a long time. This can be a difficult and uncomfortable process, but it's essential for personal growth and bringing positive change.

I am proud of my trainees and coachees for demonstrating such incredible courage in their lives. The most courageous thing they have done is to acknowledge the problem and that they needed help. It is not always an easy thing to do because it requires vulnerability and willingness to admit that you don't have all the answers. However, by acknowledging the need for help, one has already taken the first step towards a positive change. They have displayed an openness to learn, grow, and take risks, even when it means stepping out of their comfort zones and challenging the status quo.

Take Ram, for instance. Despite his fears of rejection, failure, and abuse, he was the first to make a call and apologise. It took immense courage for him to admit his mistake and take steps towards repairing the damage. Similarly, Rajesh and Priya showed tremendous bravery by changing their routines and priorities, even though it meant stepping outside of their comfort zones and embracing new challenges.

Arjun's story is also a testament to the power of courage. Despite facing criticism from family and friends, he had the strength to stand up for himself, take a step back, and work on improving his weaknesses. Vaisnavi and her mother's decision to change subjects was bold, as that required immense courage to take risks.

All journeys in this book are a testament to the power of courage and self-reflection. By acknowledging their weaknesses and working to overcome them, they have evolved to become stronger, more resilient individuals who are better equipped to navigate life's challenges.

I am honoured to have been a part of their journeys, and I look forward to seeing many such courageous journeys in each one of you. Courage is the first superpower because it makes all the others possible. Hence, courage is critical to your growth, happiness, and fulfilment.

We are not living in the caves, fighting for our lives. We live in a modern world where each day requires courage—the courage to stand up, the courage to be yourself, the courage to own your performance, the courage to hold on, and the courage to let go. Courage is standing up for your values and making bold choices. It is leaving the comfort zone for growth.

Courage is taking perspective. Courage is not only speaking and standing up for yourself but for others as well.

The superpower of courage is also a process of collecting and assessing the available information, determining the best response, making the choices that may affect you and others, and taking action to either move forward or hold back. Courage shows when you stand up, step down, or compromise for the greater good. Courage also shows when you try repeatedly and stand tall despite failures.

Mantras to Unlock Courage

1. Open Up: Most people who lack confidence fear others seeing who they truly are. Therefore, the first step is to open up and become more vulnerable. Get comfortable with others knowing the real you.
2. Understand Your Insecurities: Everyone has fears and insecurities. Admit your fears in order to overcome them. Acknowledging your insecurities will guide you to the areas that require work.
3. Face Your Fears: Your phobias and fears usually fade away after a few encounters.
4. Embrace Positivity: Practise positive self-talk. Your inner voice reveals your beliefs and thoughts. Negativity is a loop that reinforces itself, but positivity is an uphill road that requires conscious and additional effort.
5. Stress Check: Exhaustion can cause fear, so, don't stress yourself. Bite only as much as you can chew. Eat healthy, stay hydrated, exercise regularly, sleep well, and meditate. Make sure to take breaks.
6. Take Small Steps: Like every other superpower, courage comes with practise. You don't need to take a giant leap

every time, even small steps will do. Speak your heart, help people, intervene in an argument, and try to tackle the situation head-on.

7. Know Your Limits: In order to step out of your comfort zone, you need to know your limits. Push yourself to keep moving even when you face failure.
8. Have a Backup: Life is full of risks and uncertainties. Develop a backup to safeguard yourself. Build strong relationships for support and motivation, both in times of success and failure, and develop a financial backup for rainy days.
9. Do the Right Thing: Confidence, rapport, and courage are made by doing the right thing for yourself as well as for others.
10. Keep Learning: Learn new skills and improve on the existing ones. Read and talk to people for further learning. The more you know, the more courageous you will be. As Plato rightly said, 'Courage is knowing what not to fear.'
11. Embrace the Beginner Mindset: Don't aim for perfection on your first attempt when trying something new. Start with a beginner's mindset and approach everything with curiosity. Once you aim to learn, you grow.
12. Compare the Scenario: Take perspective to completely understand the scenario. Find out the worst that can happen if you take action and what you can lose if you do not. Simply comparing the two can also give you the courage to take the plunge.

A little more knowledge about the self and circumstances can fuel courage, which, in turn, boosts your success, happiness, and general well-being.

SUPERPOWER 22

ASSERTIVENESS

Do You Say No?

'To be passive is to let others decide for you. To be aggressive is to decide for others. To be assertive is to decide for yourself.'

—Edith Eva Eger

A religious guru with an impressive personality was travelling for discourse in the first-class compartment of a train. He loved smoking and wanted to smoke. There was also a quiet and humble co-passenger in his train compartment.

Pulling out a cigarette from the case with a smile on his face, Guruji said, 'I hope you won't mind me smoking?'

With his folded hands, the co-passenger humbly replied, 'Not if Guruji won't mind me getting sick.'

Self-Reflection

Recall an event from your past where you said 'yes' when you actually wanted to say no—it can be an unwanted request from family or friends or taking up more projects at work. Write about it in your Evolve Journal.

Assertiveness is a superpower that can bail you out when a person asks for a favour but you feel trapped. It can assist you when you feel guilty saying no. When you think it is difficult and uncomfortable, and when you feel like you are becoming a yes-man/woman, assertiveness helps establish boundaries.

We often say yes to any request or favour because we were taught to reply in the affirmative to any request. Every mother (the first teacher) teaches her child to say yes by explaining, 'Do what I say, don't say no!' As grown-ups, we are constantly struggling to prove ourselves in this cruel, competitive world. Thus, we say yes because, of course, it's easier to say yes!

Manisha had been struggling with assertiveness in her personal and professional relationships for a while, but it all reached a breaking point at a party one night.

Her colleagues had invited her to a loud and crowded party, but Manisha wasn't in the mood to socialise. She initially hesitated, but eventually agreed to go, sacrificing her own needs and desires.

As the night went on, Manisha felt increasingly overwhelmed and suffocated. She wasn't enjoying herself and couldn't stop thinking about what she could have done instead. Resentment towards her friends, for inviting her, and herself, for not standing up for her needs and desires, began to set in.

That's when Manisha realised she needed to learn how to be assertive and speak up for herself. She didn't want to continue feeling unhappy and resentful in her relationships, both personal and professional. She recognised that the only way to change this was to start being more confident.

Taking a deep breath to control her emotions, Manisha approached her friend and said, 'Thank you for inviting me, but I'm not enjoying myself at this party. I'm going to head out and do something else that better suits my mood.'

Her friend was surprised at first, but understood her. Manisha felt a sense of relief wash over her.

From that moment on, she started practising assertions in her personal and professional relationships. She learnt how to say no when she needed to, how to clearly express her needs and desires, and how to stand up for herself when she felt her boundaries were being crossed.

Manisha mentioned, 'It wasn't always easy, and I still have moments of doubt and insecurity. But I knew that assertiveness was the key for me to evolve.'

Through her journey of learning to be assertive, Manisha discovered the power of speaking up for oneself and creating healthy boundaries in various forms of relationships. She also realised that being assertive was not only empowering but liberating, too.

Assertiveness is the superpower of expressing what you feel, what you think, and what you opine in a way that others understand without putting their opinions, feelings, and thoughts down. Speaking up for oneself sounds easy, but it actually is difficult and uncomfortable. However, it is the ability to speak for ourselves in a way that is honest, appropriate, respectful, and direct.

By fostering the superpower of assertion, we end up building more comfortable, respectful, equitable, and fulfilling relationships, resulting in positive outcomes. Assertiveness is an effective way of expressing disagreements without confrontation. It makes us comfortable starting, continuing, and concluding a conversation.

Mantras to Unlock Assertiveness

1. Identify Your Style: Assess your natural style of communication beforehand. Is it passive-aggressive or assertive? If you say yes quickly, do you find yourself over-committing despite a lack of time and energy? Do you take on extra responsibilities? Are you a passive communicator? If your style is aggressive, are you quick to blame, reject, judge, or compliment others?
2. Think Carefully: Don't say yes or no in a rush. Take your time and pay attention to your feelings, thoughts, and opinions. You should be sure of them before committing. Please don't take too long to decide either because the longer you take, the harder it is to say no. Never take over 24 hours to make a decision.
3. Practise: If the situation makes you uncomfortable, rehearse what you want to say. Rehearsing with a general scenario can prepare you for the future.
4. Focus on 'I': Say what you feel and think is right, not what they are doing wrong. For example, say, 'In my opinion, this is not right,' instead of saying, 'What you are saying is wrong.'
5. Take Baby Steps: Start with low-risk situations. Test saying no with a friend before using it at work. Evaluate and adjust what is not working for you.
6. Express Yourself: Share your opinions with people and graciously take feedback.
7. Use Body Language: Practise some positive body language to appear confident. Make eye contact and sit or stand in a relaxed position—neither too upright and stiff nor

slouching. Neutral or positive facial expressions and body language can win half the battle.

8. Control Your Emotions: Difficult conversations can be intimidating and overwhelming. Take a deep breath and get a hold of your breathing before starting a conversation, as this will help control your emotions.
9. Listen: Assertiveness is not only about speaking for yourself but also genuinely listening.
10. Respect Your Time and Space: Set boundaries in relationships. Regard others' boundaries if you wish for them to respect yours.
11. Take Charge of Change: Things will change when you change. Practise initiating conversations if your natural style is passive. Wait for others to speak first if your conversation style is aggressive.

Saying 'no' without guilt is the first step to living a stress-free life. Learning to say it with dignity and politeness is the art that makes assertiveness a superpower.

SUPERPOWER 23

CURIOSITY

Do You Ask the Right Questions?

'It is a miracle that curiosity survives formal education.'

—Albert Einstein

Einstein is believed to have one of the highest recorded IQ scores in the world. He published hundreds of books and articles and had over 50 patents to his name. His inventions have changed how the world thinks. After he won a Nobel Prize in 1922, he was asked by a journalist, 'How are you different from your contemporaries?'

Einstein humbly responded, 'All my friends are doing well in their respective fields, and there should be no comparison of success by the number of patents and inventions.'

He continued, 'I clearly remember my childhood friends when we were studying in school. When we returned home, their mothers always asked them, "Did you have the right answers to the question today?" My mother invariably asked me, "Did you ask the right questions today?"'

'Curiosity, my friend, can make all the difference,' he concluded.

Self-Reflection

Think about how you experience curiosity across the different domains of your life. When do you feel most comfortable being curious? In what circumstances has your curiosity gotten you in trouble? What blocks or interferes with your curiosity?

The Power within the Questions

Curiosity is the strong desire to know and learn anything, show interest in ongoing experiences, find fascinating areas and topics to explore, and simply discover. Curiosity is the superpower of genius. All the discoveries happened and inventions took place because somebody was curious about them. They asked 'why' and 'why not' questions just like children—who are naturally curious.

Curious individuals are more active than passive. As they are curious, they ask questions and search for answers. This mental exercise strengthens the brain muscles, making them active and more muscular. Such people are usually more receptive to ideas and adapt quickly. They are good at decision-making, developing alternative approaches to suit various situations, communication, and discussion abilities. All this makes them great team players—both at work and at home.

I remember meeting Sonia when she was feeling stuck in her life. She had become overly focused on being productive and getting things done, which made her lose touch with her sense of curiosity. She was good at her job, but she wasn't passionate about it. She was aware that something was amiss. She needed to learn how to approach problems in new ways.

Together, we identified the areas of Sonia's life where she could be more curious. I helped her set goals for herself and encouraged her to start small. She read books on topics that interested her and attended various workshops and seminars. She also pursued new hobbies, such as painting and cooking, to expand her horizons.

At first, Sonia was hesitant. She was used to being practical and productive, and she wasn't sure if trying out new things like reading, journalling, and painting could help her. She was hesitant also because she didn't want to be a laughing stock by asking questions. But when I pushed her to try it out for a while, she decided to explore and expand her horizons. We started with what she was more comfortable with, such as goal-setting, reflecting, and digital fasting.

With these small changes, something inside Sonia changed. She became better connected to the people and things around her. She found herself approaching problems in new ways. She was now fully committed—reading books and articles, journalling, pursuing her hobby of painting, and, above all, asking questions, no matter how serious or silly.

Years later, I was amazed to see Sonia on social media as a fashion blogger and influencer. The new, curious Sonia was challenging herself to learn more and grow in new ways. When you use this superpower wisely, you become a happier, more evolved version of yourself.

Mantras to Unlock Curiosity

1. Do What You Love: Discover your passion. When you do things that you genuinely enjoy, curiosity comes naturally.
2. Ask Questions: Questions can unlock any conversation. So, ask questions—a lot of them. It doesn't matter if they

are silly. Questions can keep you and others interested in a conversation. Also make sure to ask open questions, as they provide the speaker with ample choices. Ask questions to probe further—what, why, when, who, where, and how.

3. Keep an Open Mind: Take perspective, talk to others, and discuss their points of view. Don't start a discussion with assumptions; keep them open. People feel comfortable talking to those who are warm and welcoming.
4. Get Uncomfortable: The creative juices run dry in familiar, predictable settings. Step out of your comfort zone, get uncomfortable, and take a leap in unfamiliar, unpredictable environments.
5. Be Mindful: The world outside is full of amazing things. Just be mindful and start exploring them. Ask questions like, 'Why does the rose have thorns?' 'Why do the leaves of different trees have different shapes?'
6. Do a Digital Detox: These days, we often look for answers to everything in technology. Find your answers without technology. Pursue your childhood hobby—draw your dream home from childhood—or cook an old family recipe. Refrain from using technology for performing any of these tasks.
7. Learn New Skills: Use it or lose it—this is true for all the muscles of the body, including brain muscles. Muscles develop with use, and exercising your brain muscles by learning new skills strengthens them. Look at the geniuses around you—they have diverse interests.
8. Reflect: Thinking about your past and asking questions can also help. Reflect on a job that you find boring. Pay attention to at least three or more novel features of that job. Reflect and challenge your ideas and thoughts and

give powerful arguments to oppose your initial ideas. This habit of reflection will develop empathy, building firm beliefs as you have thought it all.

Choose to be curious. Enjoy being curious. Break free from the rut. Observe what this superpower adds to your life. Master the art of asking the right questions to unlock the bounteous possibilities.

SUPERPOWER 24

PERSPECTIVE-TAKING

Do You Look beyond the Obvious?

'Everything we hear is an opinion, not a fact. Everything we see is a perspective, not the truth.'
—Marcus Aurelius

There lived a brilliant and kind king. But he had a disability—he was missing one leg and one eye. His kingdom was flourishing, and he was satisfied with his past performances and vision for the future. Despite all this, something was bothering him. He felt like he was missing something.

One day, he was passing through the palace hallway and saw portraits of his ancestors on the wall. He wondered, *How will people remember me when I am gone? How will my lineage recognise me?* His thoughts continued, *I don't want to look terrible in my portrait. I only have one leg and one eye. My portrait will be laughed upon!*

As soon as the kingdom's prime minister understood the cause of his king's worry, he invited famous painters to paint his beautiful portrait to be hung on the wall of fame of the kingdom. He added, 'Anyone who can do this will get a reward beyond imagination.'

The painters were in a conundrum. They wondered, 'With one leg and one eye, how can the portrait look beautiful? How can his picture be made exquisite? If the picture doesn't look good, the king will surely punish us.' None of the skilled painters agreed to take the job.

'I will make a wonderful portrait of the King . . . as beautiful as my King is,' said an amateur painter. Everyone was curious about the final painting. The question on everyone's mind was, 'How will he do it?'

The painter promised to return with the painting in a month.

A month later, everyone was waiting for him. People were curious and nervous. The painter confidently presented his art to the King, leaving everyone stunned.

The painting portrayed the king sitting on a horse, taking aim at some prey. The profile the painter chose established a flattering perspective of the King as he was sitting on the horse—making only one leg visible and one eye closed as he was taking aim. The king was delighted and thoroughly impressed by the painter. He was awarded an advisory role as his courtier, as promised, simply because he had the superpower to look beyond the obvious and find a different perspective.

Self-Reflection

Sit comfortably, relax, and take a few deep breaths. When your breathing becomes regular, imagine yourself on your deathbed. Imagine who all are there and what they are talking about.

If this seems difficult, consider a conflict situation with your loved one. Reflect on how a neutral third party, who wants the best for all, would view this argument. Jot down your reflections in the Evolve Journal.

It's All in Your Mind

Perspective is the superpower of looking beyond yourself. It is seeing and understanding the world from others' vantage points—how others think and feel in particular situations. People who possess, nurture, and cultivate this superpower are usually wise, can counsel others, and see the bigger picture.

I was the head of a private business school when we received the news that the university's legal status was in jeopardy due to a decision made by the Supreme Court. Some of my colleagues immediately left their jobs, while others were unsure of what to do. As we deliberated, tensions rose, and the students became increasingly restless.

Before we knew it, we were in the midst of a violent protest. Some students began pelting stones, others started sloganeering, and chaos was rampant. We knew we had to act quickly to avoid a potentially disastrous outcome. Working with some of the student leaders, we managed to calm the situation and put an end to the violence.

But the aftermath left us with mixed emotions—fear, anger, frustration, and insecurity. Some of us wondered if we should even be concerned about the students who had thrown the stones, and some others were still uncertain about the best course of action. It was clear that we needed to take a step back and look at the situation from a more balanced perspective.

The next day, we all agreed that we needed to find a way to navigate the situation and ensure that the students were not left out in the cold. We also knew that communication was essential. So, we started by encouraging them to talk, while we listened patiently to their concerns.

Then, we explained the situation from our perspective and talked about the possibilities and options. Throughout the entire conversation, we made sure that we were not influenced by any biases or the sloganeering and stone-pelting experience.

Ultimately, the college administration and students decided to work together. We approached local universities and administration for support, and the students mounted pressure through the media. It was a challenging time, and there were moments of uncertainty and doubt, but we remained committed to finding a solution, no matter how difficult the road ahead might be.

In the end, our efforts paid off, and we were able to find a solution that protected the students' interests. This experience taught us that taking perspective is a win-win game. Empathy, collaboration, communication, and staying calm and composed are the mantras of acknowledging different viewpoints. It's crucial to be aware of our biases and emotions and take a step back to objectively analyse the situation. Only then can we find the best way forward.

Perspective also provides a clear picture of our situation(s). When we experience stress for significant periods, it can create a negative bias. We start focusing on the worst-case scenarios—what is not going right and what is missing. This bias can make us feel like everything around us is going haywire and out of our control. In such situations, the superpower of taking perspective aids in finding meaning and happiness.

Make sure you don't annoy others by giving them your perspective and advice without them seeking it. Moreover, you do yourself an injustice when you overburden yourself with the issues, secrets, and challenges of others. Take perspective to examine the world that makes sense to yourself and others. Your perspective shapes your reality. Changing your perspective can alter your reality.

Mantras to Unlock Perspective-Taking

1. Be Curious: Whenever talking to others, let go of your ego and listen actively with an open mind. Seek to understand their viewpoints, feelings, emotions, thoughts, values, and understanding of the situation. Ask 'why' at least five times or till you get an answer you can easily grasp.
2. Put Your Feelings Aside: Consciously put your emotions aside and focus on others' perspectives.
3. Remove Bias: Our biases are significant obstacles to taking perspective. When you attempt to take perspective, take care of acknowledging your bias as well.
4. Share Your Feelings: All feelings and emotions are valid, so, talk openly about them in order to understand the situation better.
5. Respect Everyone's Feelings: No emotion or feeling is evil—not even sadness, anger, or loneliness. Acknowledge and respect what you are feeling as well as what others might be feeling. When you acknowledge them honestly, you understand others' perspectives better.
6. Ideate: Using the information about them—their feelings, moods, backgrounds, intentions, expectations, etc.—imagine how someone would perceive the world and their reactions to different situations.

7. Anticipate: When you have ideas, narrow them down. Make the best guesses you possibly can. Anticipate their likely reactions. Hypothesise—if this is true, what should I expect? If this is wrong—what will be the outcome? The real situation may not look exactly like your hypothesis but strive to be as close as you possibly can.
8. Adjust: Look at the other side and ask 'what if' questions. Observe and adjust your perspectives when they deviate, especially when there is new information. Both your hypothesis and perspective can change.
9. Validate: While you may disagree with someone's perspective, it's important to validate your own understanding by paraphrasing what you think their position to be.
10. Create an Encouraging Environment: People open up quickly in a warm environment. Make them comfortable both before and during the conversation. Use encouragers while they are talking.

Taking perspective is a win-win game. This superpower makes you a better thinker and communicator. It also makes you a better friend, family member, and colleague.

SUPERPOWER 25

CREATIVITY

Are You Confined in a Box?

Creativity involves breaking out of established patterns in order to look at things in a different way.'
—Edward de Bono

A long time ago, near Darjeeling, India, lived a wise, hardworking comb merchant named Badri, who had built a business empire of his own. When he fell gravely ill, he realised it was time to hand over the business to capable hands.

Badri had three sons. He decided to check their mettle before choosing his successor. He held a test, wherein he informed his sons, 'One who will sell the most combs in the nearby Buddhist Monastery in three days will inherit my business.'

The sons were confused as monks didn't have hair. They wondered, *What to do? What will a monk use a comb for? This is insane.*

Three days later, the eldest son sold two combs to the monks as a back-scratching tool. The youngest sold fifteen combs by advising the monks to keep combs in the monastery for visitors and pilgrims who mostly came from faraway places. The third son, Subodh, was running late. As his brothers mocked him, Subodh rushed in saying, 'Sorry, I am late. I am coming here after delivering fifteen hundred combs to the monastery.'

The brothers and the father were surprised by this number.

'Good job! But how did you do it? Did you trick the monks with tall tales?' asked the man.

'No, I have not tricked the monks. I just gave them an idea,' Subodh responded.

'What idea?'

'The idea was that they could give away combs printed with Buddhist wisdom at the souvenir store. Visitors and pilgrims could buy these as souvenirs, which will help them remind of the Buddhist wisdom daily.'

He added, 'I was late because the printing job took time!'

Self-Reflection

Reflect on your creative side and rank your creative self on a scale of 1–10 (one being the lowest). Now think about what creativity can do for you. Take note of your reflections in the Evolve Journal.

Growth Is Outside the Box

I was conducting training sessions on creativity and innovation at Sashastra Seema Bal Academy, Chandukhedi, Bhopal. The participants were DIGs (Deputy Inspector General) and this was mandatory training for their promotion.

During one exercise, I asked the participants to come up with as many solutions as they could to divide a square into four equal parts. To my surprise, and more to theirs, all the participants came up with identical solutions in the same sequence. It was a sign that they were thinking similarly and needed to enhance their creativity skills.

To help them think more creatively, we did a few more exercises, post which I introduced the Six Thinking Hats® technique. I wanted them to apply this method to a real-life scenario, so I presented the problem of whether to build a playground or a swimming pool in their housing society. I reiterated they should stick to a specific mindset and must not stop themselves even if their point appears to be silly.

I started by wearing the White Hat, presenting the facts and figures related to building each facility, including the estimated cost of construction, maintenance, and repair, the number of residents who would use each facility, and the expected return on investment for each option.

Then, I put on the Red Hat, encouraging the participants to think emotionally and share their feelings about the two options. Some participants felt that a swimming pool would be more enjoyable for the residents, while others thought that a playground would be a safer and family-friendly option.

Next, I wore the Black Hat and asked the participants to think about the potential risks and drawbacks of each option. Some participants highlighted the safety concerns and insurance implications of building a swimming pool, while others pointed out the maintenance challenges of a playground.

Then, I put on the Yellow Hat and urged the participants to think about the benefits of each option. Some participants emphasised the social and developmental benefits of a playground, while others highlighted the recreational benefits of a swimming pool.

After that, I wore the Green Hat and encouraged the participants to brainstorm new ideas and solutions. Some participants suggested building a combined facility that included both a playground and a swimming pool, while others proposed incorporating other amenities like a gym or a community centre.

Finally, I wore the Blue Hat and summarised the key points we had discussed. We considered all the information gathered and weighed the pros and cons of each option. Ultimately, we arrived at a decision that was informed by a range of perspectives and considered the needs and preferences of all stakeholders.

By the end of the training session, the participants were confident that they could enhance their creativity using the tools and techniques provided. They were convinced that creativity was essential for problem-solving, both in their professional and personal lives. The session was a success, and the feedback received from the participants was overwhelmingly positive, with many expressing their affirmation to apply creativity to their work and personal lives.

Lack of everyday creativity is true for most of us. We fear being creative at least in a formal set-up because most of us associate creativity with having fun, being an artist or a craftworker, or something involving a creative process. We associate it with people who are in the process of creating or innovating something. Even the dictionaries never miss to mention the word 'creation' about defining creativity. Creativity is not limited to just creation; its length, breadth, and scope in its entirety are infinite.

Creativity is the superpower to perceive the existing world around us with new lenses. It connects the dots in apparently unrelated events and finds unusual patterns. Creativity is imagining the what ifs and why nots. It is about listening to your gut and answering questions that are not even asked.

Creativity helps us in all walks of life because it is about finding new ways to approach the same situation and solve problems. It is not confined only to those who are into making art, innovating, or involved in any other so-called creative processes. Creativity is not a legacy of right-brained thinkers; it is a superpower anyone can possess and benefit from.

Only creativity motivates us to knock on the untapped potential of our personality, career, business, relationships, success, and happiness. Our world without creativity is only a box of outdated ideas and solutions. Creativity helps us break free from conventional thinking and grow boundlessly.

Mantras to Unlock Creativity

1. Adopt a Fresh Perspective: Look at things from a fresh angle, and record the difference in detail. These details will fuel your creativity. Notice the difference you see, feel, taste, hear, or touch.
2. Unlearn the Familiar: When you want a new solution, forget what you did in the past, and start from zero. For instance, if a baker attempts to innovate a cake with a presumption that it has to be sweet and gentle, they are putting themselves in a box. Outside this box lies the possibility of creating bitter, hot, or citrusy cakes.
3. Speak Your Mind: Do not analyse and brainstorm simultaneously. Set aside some time to think of as many ideas as possible, whether silly or brilliant, fresh or stale, new or old. If it's in your mind, pen it down. Evaluate the merits and demerits only after that time is over.

4. Start with a Positive: If it's not your idea and you want to critique it, start with the positives first. Study the potential challenges you face. This deliberation provides a fair chance to both the idea and the proposer; otherwise, the thought and creativity are killed too soon.
5. Form Connections: Creativity is all about establishing new connections. Practise making connections between random things, ideas, and concepts. For example, take two unrelated things or words and find a common thread.
6. Daydream: Take some time out from your routine and sit idly, stare at the fan and let your thoughts wander. Have a hot bath or a cold shower. Relax and allow your mind to meander.
7. Move Around: If you feel stuck, get up, take a walk or dance around. Exercising is another way of getting the creative juices flowing.
8. Exercise Your Brain: Brain muscles increase when stirred. Stimulation for the brain lies in randomness, surprises, challenges, provocation, and dissent. One can achieve all this simply by breaking the monotony in life—such as visiting a friend without an appointment, taking an unusual route to the office, sleeping on the other side of the bed, using your non-dominant hand for daily chores, trying new cuisine, disagreeing with a friend, wearing a colour you would otherwise never imagine wearing, or going on an adventurous trip.
9. Surrender the First Choice: This is the most impressive and doable of all. Whenever you are solving a problem or facing a situation, never do what comes up as the first choice in your mind as your default approach and seek the next one.

10. Thinking Hats: Edward de Bono has provided us with an excellent technique of Six Thinking Hats® to look at the situation from six perspectives. After wearing these hats, one can have plenty of ideas to compare.

    Black Hat: Look at only the negatives—what is not going to work?

    Blue Hat: Look at the bigger picture—what is the best overall solution?

    Green Hat: Look for creativity—what are the alternatives?

    Red Hat: Look at the emotional side—what is your gut feeling?

    White Hat: Look at the facts objectively—what are they?

    Yellow Hat: Look at the positives only—what will definitely work?

Dare to be creative because wherever creativity exists, success eventually follows. Cultivate this superpower, encourage it and shine.

SUPERPOWER 26

PRUDENCE

Give it a Second Thought

'Prudence is a necessary ingredient in all the virtues, without which they degenerate into folly and excess.'

—Jeremy Collier

A merchant once saw two miserable vultures in the water. He took them with him, fed them some meat, and put them in a dry corner of a slaughterhouse near his place. The vultures eventually flew back to the mountains after the rains. They felt indebted to the kind merchant and resolved to thank him by gifting him clothes. These vultures would fly every day from house to house and village to village to steal clothes drying in the sun and offer them to the merchant. Though the merchant appreciated the vultures' intent, he did not use those clothes. Instead, he kept them carefully in a safe place.

The villagers were upset and complained about their clothes being stolen by the vultures. The king ordered his subjects to capture the vultures. A few days later, they caught one of the vultures and presented it to the king who asked, 'Why are you stealing from my people?'

The bird replied, 'One fateful day, a merchant saved me and my brother, so we are collecting these clothes to give them as our token of gratitude.'

The king called the merchant for questioning.

'Sir,' he said, 'the vultures did bring me many clothes, but I haven't used them. I kept all the clothes safely to return them to their owners someday.'

The king pardoned the vultures considering the intention of the act. The merchant was also spared as the king appreciated his prudence.

Self-Reflection

Ponder upon your decision-making skills. Do you think before acting, speaking, and deciding? Do you make decisions quickly or calmly? Do you lie or cheat about trivial things? Make a note of these answers in your Evolve Journal.

The First Thought Is Just a Feeling

As the new head of the department at the college, I knew that I had my work cut out for me. My boss, Devraj, had a reputation for being impulsive and making decisions without considering the consequences. Though I connected with him instantly, I could see why several of my colleagues found it difficult to work with him, and some even feared losing their jobs due to his unpredictable nature.

Despite his reputation, I always approached Devraj with an open mind and a willingness to work together. I listened to his concerns and discussed different perspectives, and slowly but surely, a rapport was developed between us. Soon enough, I was one of his core team members, and he valued my input and ideas.

One day, while discussing Indian mythology, I quoted a lesson from the ancient scriptures: 'Don't promise when happy, don't speak when angry and don't decide when sad.' Devraj was a well-read and educated man, and this resonated with him deeply and I could see a sudden realisation dawning on him. I had hit the chord with him, and he shared that he had been making impulsive decisions without giving much thought to the consequences and that he needed to be more mindful and prudent in his approach.

Devraj realised the importance of prudence and started to apply it in his decision-making. He began to take a step back and think twice before making any decisions. He realised that his impulsive behaviour was making the college's overall environment hostile. He became more open to feedback and suggestions, at least from his core team, and everyone else could sense a shift in his leadership style.

In the end, all our team efforts paid off, as our college's performance and environment improved. Through this experience, I learnt that anyone can be a coach or mentor if they have the right mindset and approach. One does not necessarily need a formal title or career to make a positive impact; sometimes, just being a supportive colleague or friend can make a huge difference. It just takes the willingness of both parties to listen, reflect, and adapt.

Prudence is often confused with stuffiness and rigidity. Slow and overly cautious individuals are not prudent or those who don't trust anyone and are always worried about the future.

Prudence is the superpower that rationalises desire with reason. It is the superpower to restrain and resist, the superpower that helps us manage our habits and protect us against an excess of anything. Prudence means being careful and giving a second thought while speaking, listening, and watching. Prudence is resisting impulsive decision-making or jumping to conclusions. It involves stopping and thinking before acting on anything.

Prudent individuals refrain from taking unnecessary risks and from saying or performing actions they would regret later. They are the ones who possess the power of anticipation, as they are reflective and act with cautious knowledge.

Consequently, prudence is the superpower that objectively helps us consider the after-effects of our actions, as well as aids in resisting or encouraging the action(s) based on these reflections.

Mantras to Unlock Prudence

1. Learn from Your and Others' Mistakes: Reflect on your mistakes by asking yourself these questions: How did I perceive the situation? What were my options of action or inaction? What was in my control? Where did I go wrong in my actions or words? What can I improve next time? Also analyse others' mistakes and learn from them.
2. Think Twice: Think twice before acting and reacting. While making a decision, consider the consequences and if you are ready to live with them. When something or someone pushes your buttons, restrain your reaction and respond after giving it a second thought.
3. Gain Insight: See whether you are reacting to your emotions or responding to the facts and evidence. make it a point to look at the situation from different perspectives.
4. Plan Your Future: Make contingency strategies while planning for the future. If plan A fails, one should have plans B, C, D, and so on. One must make corresponding plans for both the present and future when planning

for tomorrow. Test yourself using the if/then line of questioning. For instance: If I want to eat out every day, then I must forgo the month-end vacation plan. If I wish for a month-end vacation, then I must stop eating out frequently.

5. Resist and Restrain: Restrain decision-making when you are angry, stressed, worried, tired, or depressed. Also, avoid making promises when you are happy. Make them only when you are relaxed and comfortable.
6. Consult: When in doubt, consult your trusted friends, family, or significant others for insight.

Prudence is not suspending decisions or actions, nor is it about avoiding responsibilities. It simply means responsibly taking decisions after considering everything and taking the best possible course.

SUPERPOWER 27

CRITICAL THINKING

How Do You Think?

'If you judge people, you have no time to love them.'
—Mother Teresa

Pointing at the trees outside her window, a 24-year-old girl shouted, 'Mom, look at the trees. They are moving!'

Her mother was happy. She just smiled and nodded her head. A young couple sitting next to them looked at the girl with pity as she suddenly exclaimed, 'Mom, see, the clouds are chasing us!'

The mother stroked her head and smiled again. The couple could not resist this time and asked, 'Why don't you take her to a good doctor?'

The mother replied, 'I did. We are just returning home after her successful eye implant surgery. You see, she was blind from birth.'

Self-Reflection

Reflect and pinpoint at least three past events when you did not think through your actions and later regretted being judgemental. Make a note in your Evolve Journal.

Organise, Analyse, and Rationalise

Judgment is the superpower to make well-informed decisions, create objective opinions, and reach rational conclusions based on knowledge, experiences, and personal qualities. It involves thinking through and examining things, and being free from assumptions, conclusions, and beliefs. It also means not being rigid, as well as weighing the information and options fairly, not jumping to conclusions, and changing one's mind if required in light of available information and evidence.

Geeta was in a vulnerable position when I met her for the first time. I could sense that she was struggling to find her way and make the right decisions for herself. It was clear that her decision to marry Abhi without her parents' consent was just the beginning of a series of wrong choices that would haunt her for years to come.

Geeta and Abhi had been married for seven years, and for the most part, things had been seemingly good between them. They were happy and supportive of each other's careers. However, an unexpected pregnancy changed everything. The doctors informed Geeta that her pregnancy was risky, but she and Abhi decided to proceed with it regardless. Geeta had to quit her job to take care of herself, and Abhi took a promotion and transfer to prepare for their upcoming responsibilities.

Sadly, Geeta miscarried, and it was devastating for both. She believed that Abhi was just struggling to cope with the trauma of losing a child, but over time, it became clear that there were deeper issues at play. Geeta kept trying to conceive, thinking it would fix everything, but it only made things worse.

Years later, after several medical interventions, when Geeta finally conceived for the second time, she discovered that Abhi had been cheating on her for a while. She was shocked and hurt, however, she still tried to hold onto the hope that things could work in their favour. She gave birth to their daughter, and for a while, they pretended that everything was okay between them. However, Geeta soon realised that she was being used by Abhi and his family. She was living with her in-laws and taking care of their child, while Abhi was living with the other woman.

That's when I met Geeta. She had started working with me, and we talked extensively about her decision to get a divorce. It was a tough decision because it meant letting Abhi off the hook for his responsibilities, and Geeta had no financial backing to support herself and her daughter.

Together, we worked on building her confidence, and I asked Geeta to reflect on her decision and think critically about what getting a divorce meant for her future. I encouraged her to weigh the pros and cons of the decision and consider factors like her personal goals, values, overall well-being, and her daughter's future.

Geeta began by asking herself important questions like, 'What are my reasons for wanting a divorce?' 'What are the potential consequences of this decision on me and my daughter?' 'Am I well-equipped to face these consequences?' She also asked a lot of what-if questions, such as what if things didn't turn out as planned? She even played devil's advocate for her daughter's perspective.

After much reflection, Geeta realised that getting a divorce was the best option for her and her happiness. She was confident in her choice because she had taken the time to think critically about what it would mean for herself and her daughter.

As she went through the process of a divorce and moving on from her marriage, I noticed that her improved critical thinking skills had not only helped her make a sound decision, but it had also provided her with a sense of clarity and empowerment.

Today, Geeta is doing great. She's thriving in the education industry and raising a responsible and happy teenage daughter who loves to bake and dance—my heart was full when she baked a cake for me on my birthday last year! It makes me happy to see how far she's come, and I am glad that I could be of help.

Critical thinking relates to the process of decision-making. While it doesn't guarantee good results, it makes sure if the decision is not the best, at least, it is the least harmful one. This either enhances the odds of success or reduces the loss. According to the Bhagavad Gita, Chapter 2, Verse 47:

Karmanye vadhikaraste Ma Phaleshu Kadachana.
Ma Karmaphalaheturbhurma Te Sangostvakarmani.

It conveys that you only have rights and control over the action, but never over the fruit of that action. Only focus on the process (action) being right, and don't get distracted by or attached to the result.

Good judgment is vital in decision-making. It helps make choices and decisions regarding everyday things. Thus, this superpower is essential for everyone at all stages of life. Some experts define critical thinking as a gut feeling, a subconscious ability to recognise patterns. But to my understanding, critical thinking is the ability to integrate what you are born with and what you have learnt in your formative years to make good decisions and appropriate choices. This is a skill that can both be learnt and honed.

Every moment, we are constantly thinking about events, things, and people. Critical thinking kicks in when we consciously employ our intellectual gears in a particular fashion to make more accurate choices.

The process of critical thinking involves six steps:

i. Learn and gather as much information as possible. No matter how much we struggle, the information we have is imperfect.
ii. Check the quality of the collected information. Identify and explore trusted and diverse sources of information. Evaluate the trustworthiness of the source.
iii. Reflect on your experiences—what went right or wrong, and in what situations?iv. Understand your values and biases. Use your values and avoid biases when appropriate.
v. Explore and examine the options. If you cannot spot options or choices, revoke your decision and start over. Take more time to gather your thoughts or wait for more information.
vi. Implement the decision within the appropriate context. A good decision can fail if the person implementing it does not grasp the context. The same decision can have different outcomes in different contexts.

All these stages require various skills, and improving upon them can improve your judgment and critical thinking.

Mantras to Unlock Critical Thinking

1. Ask the Right Questions: Know precisely what you are looking for by identifying the problem and objective for the judgment. What do you want out of the situation? Be curious and ask questions of who, why, what, when, where, and how.
2. Question Your Bias: Consciously reflect on your past decisions and identify your unconscious preferences and motivations that influenced your choices. Aim at finding patterns. Identify your biases and question how they influence your judgment. Be aware of biases while making a decision.
3. Reflect on the Basic Assumptions: Question the assumptions for better judgment. The world's greatest inventors simply said, 'What if?' and challenged their general beliefs, and proved everyone wrong.
4. Play the Devil's Advocate: A good decision supports your point of view or the popular point of view. It might also go against your way of looking at things. Consider the evidence against the dominant views and then arrive at a decision.
5. Be Self-Aware: Self-aware individuals are better equipped to make sound judgments. Learn about your biases, assumptions, beliefs, values, and prejudices. Keep yourself open to feedback. Accept and take responsibility for your mistakes.
6. Use Your Knowledge: Experience is integral to decision-making. Use it wisely. Reiterate what went well and prevent repeating what did not.
7. Automate Routine: The mind gets fatigued with a lot of decisions. Keep your mind off and automate repeating and

routine decision-making. Use that mental space for more important decision-making instead. For example, plan a weekly menu instead of doing it daily.

8. Consider the Consequences: Every option has consequences for you as well as others. Weigh the consequences by writing down the pros and cons of each available option. This will help give you a clear picture.
9. Evaluate All Information: Any available information should be taken with a pinch of salt. Not all information is usable, so always ask questions like, 'Is this information complete and up to date?' 'Are there any missing ends?' or 'How reliable is the source?'
10. Practise Active Listening: Actively listen to all the people and voices, understand their perspectives, recognise their biases, empathise with them, and acknowledge their preferences.
11. Avoid Overthinking: Recognise the fine line between critical thinking and overthinking. Sometimes, the easiest solution is the optimum solution. Don't get stuck with research and reading so much that you either stop thinking or start overthinking.
12. Recognise Your Inability to Always Think Critically: Critical thinking is a tool that should be used according to needs. You don't need critical thinking for every decision—it is required only for making important decisions and difficult choices. Despite following the process and practising critical thinking, lapses of judgement and slip-ups can occur. The intention is to minimise them in the future.

Critical thinking, though a vital skill, is not easy. The mantras may sound simple, but they are not. They pay off only when there is an open mindset to entertain diversity and the flexibility to embrace change. Regular practise is the key to honing this superpower.

SUPERPOWER 28

LEARNING

Do You Sharpen Your Saw?

'Arise, awake, and stop not till the goal is reached.'
—Swami Vivekananda

Once upon a time, there were two woodcutter friends named Ram and Shyam. They had a bittersweet relationship because of their distinct personalities. Ram was funny, fast, and furious. Shyam was sober, calm, and cautious. Every morning, they used to go to the forest together to chop wood. Every evening, at the village chaupal, Ram used to crack jokes about Shyam's cautious and slow mannerisms. Shyam often told stories about their experiences in the forest.

One day, a wise man in the village suggested they have a competition to determine who is better at woodcutting. They both agreed enthusiastically. The rules were simple—it would be fair play, they would only use their manual axes, and the quantity of wood collected in a day would decide the winner.

The next morning both wished each other luck and headed to the forest in the spirit of the game. They chose their own stretches to chop and started chopping the wood at the fastest speed possible. Both were working like their usual self. Shyam, being calm and cautious, was chopping and stopping to rest, then chopping again. Ram was determined to win so he kept chopping without any breaks. He confidently shouted, 'I am the winner!'

However, much to Ram's shock, Shyam had chopped a lot more wood than him.

Furious, he remarked, 'How is this possible? I saw you resting every hour, whereas I was tirelessly cutting the woods all day.'

Shyam calmly replied, 'Yes, my dear friend, I was stopping every hour. While you were relentlessly chopping the wood, I was stopping and sharpening my saw.'

Self-Reflection

Are you enthusiastic about learning new things? What conscious efforts have you made in the last week to learn anything new? What have you learnt in the previous month and year? Note down your reflections in the Evolve Journal.

Learning Never Ceases

As a trainer, Sheena was skilled in her role, but being a new entrant to the workforce, she lacked some fundamental New Age skills such as PowerPoint and Excel. It was surprising to discover that she wasn't very enthusiastic about learning these skills, nor was she actively seeking out new challenges and learning opportunities.

To help her develop a growth mindset and take a more proactive approach to her learning, I started by asking

Sheena questions about her career goals and the additional skills she would need to achieve those goals. We discussed the importance of continuous learning and the return on investment of learning those skills in terms of time, money, and energy. This exercise was eye-opening for Sheena, and it helped her understand the value of self-directed and continuous learning.

That point onwards, we started small by encouraging her to read books, blogs, and articles, watch self-learning videos, participate in events and conferences, and engage in online forums and communities. We also identified her learning style and introduced her to new tools and techniques for self-directed learning, such as online courses, podcasts, and webinars.

Over time, Sheena's learning skills significantly improved, and, as a result, she began taking on more challenging projects and responsibilities at work. As her confidence grew in her abilities, she started seeing herself not just as a trainer but a lifelong learner, constantly seeking new opportunities to improve her skills and knowledge.

With a little support and guidance, Sheena embraced a growth mindset, and her career advanced drastically as she continued to develop her learning and professional skills.

Learning is the superpower required to acquire new skills, topics, and bodies of knowledge. This learning, unlearning, and relearning can either be formal or self-motivated. It is an extension of the superpower 'curiosity' as it goes beyond simply being curious to making a self-motivated effort to learn more. It is a superpower to admire the opportunity to seek out, hold on to, and deepen simply for the joy of learning.

Learning never stops as minds are curious. Consciously or subconsciously, we are constantly learning to keep up with the changing world around us. If this learning process is intentional, the benefits derived can be rewarding. Furthermore, in this age, information is readily available at our fingertips, making learning much easier. If one has the will, this superpower removes all limits to learning—reading, formal classes, watching videos, television, friends, family, etc.

Learning new things keeps you relevant in an ever-changing environment. It opens up several opportunities to explore your calling. Those who readily learn skills are more adaptable in nature. In this dynamic, fast-paced world, learning new skills is no more a choice but a necessity.

Mantras to Unlock Learning

1. Unlearn: You must need to unlearn what you think you know so that you learn what you need to know. Unlearning is the first step towards acquiring new skills. The Covid-19 pandemic made unlearning and relearning more relevant than ever before. Individuals who are ignorant in the times ahead will not be those who cannot read and write, but those who cannot learn, unlearn, and relearn.
2. Ask Questions: Our growth is limited by the questions we ask and not by the answers we know. Be curious to find new opportunities for learning, unlearning, and relearning.
3. Be Humble: Being humble is the most crucial aspect of learning. Accept that there are things you may not know, things you may not do well, and things you may be doing incorrectly.
4. Embrace Discomfort: Change is always uncomfortable, so it's essential to rid yourself of the mindset of 'I know it all'. Alter your existing ways of doing and learning things to

change your perspective. Get ready to embrace discomfort to become a better you.

5. Prepare Yourself: Set your learning goal and assess it on the SMART (specific, measurable, achievable, realistic, time-bound) scale. Consider how much and how many resources, time, and money are required, and how much you are willing to spend. Fully commit yourself.
6. Focus on Relational Learning: Relating new lessons to the things you already know makes it easier to learn and retain things.
7. Check Your Return on Investment: Learning new skills is hard work. Before you commit, make sure it's worth it. Ask yourself, 'Will this benefit my career or personal life in the long run?' Unless it is relevant or sponsored, don't randomly invest your time, money, energy, or other resources. It is an investment, so assess your return on it as well.
8. Identify the Barriers: Identify potential challenges and obstacles you can face while learning a new skill—time, energy, finance, travel, or anything else. Note down the motivators, such as increased income, promotion, and status. Look at them together to find practical ways to aid your learning.
9. Learn in Multiple Ways: People learn differently—some learn better by seeing, some by hearing, some by reading, some by coaching, and some by experimenting. However, most of us learn in multiple ways. Figure out your style by reflecting on your past learning experiences and make a list of the good and bad ones. Recognise the commonalities among the good ones and identify similar missing elements in the bad ones. It is wise to use more than one sense in learning.

10. Seek Help: Find an expert who can give you honest feedback after judging your progress. However, it's advisable to not choose your immediate superior for this role.
11. Start Small: Don't attempt to do everything at once. Choose one or two skills at a time, set your learning goals, and split the big goal into bite-sized pieces so that it doesn't become overwhelming. For instance, if you're focusing on time management, begin by making your to-do list daily.
12. Track Your Progress: Keep track of your progress from time to time. Discuss it with your friends and family, as they can provide you with feedback and inform you if you are moving in the right direction. Talking to people will also motivate you and make you feel more accountable.
13. Discover Additional Practice Opportunities: Teaching others the skill you are learning will surely cement your learning better. Teaching others is also beneficial for practice. While teaching, you will answer many questions and clarify the confusion. Explaining and answering these will make your understanding firmer.
14. Take Your Time: Nobody can learn skills overnight, so it's important to keep calm and avoid rushing. Practise consistently, and progress will automatically occur. Sometimes, it can take about six months to master a skill, and even longer for it to be evident to the rest of the world.
15. Learn from Mistakes: Making mistakes is an essential learning tool, so don't hesitate to make them. While learning a skill, knowing what not to do is more crucial than knowing what to do. Mistakes indicate progress, as they add one more item to the list of things to not do.

16. Learn Regularly: Make learning new skills a regular practice. Continued learning will keep the brain active and ready to receive.

The success of learning lies with you. Open your mind, embrace change, and challenge yourself to let go and unlearn what you think you know so that you can learn and relearn what you need to know. Keep the motto of 'Learn to unlearn before you relearn' close to your heart.

SUPERPOWER 29

FOCUS

Know What Not to Do

'For those who have conquered the mind, it is their friend. For those who have failed to do so, the mind works like an enemy.'

—Bhagavad Gita

One day, Swami Vivekananda was walking along the shores of a river in Chicago, USA. He saw some little boys standing on the bridge with air guns, aiming to shoot floating eggshells on the river. The eggshells were bobbing up and down with the constant movement of the water, making the boys miss each shot.

Vivekananda was watching this unfold closely when one boy asked, 'Do you want to try?'

Swami Vivekananda took the air gun and shot twelve rounds. Each one of them hit an eggshell. The boys were amazed and asked, 'Wow! How did you do that?'

Swami Vivekananda replied, 'I have never tried shooting before. How did I do it? Well, two words: Focus and concentration. Whatever you do, concentrate on that one thing. When you aim, your focus should only be on the target, nothing else. Focus all your senses on that one thing you are doing at that moment. When you shoot, put your heart and mind only on the target. When you're learning, put your heart and mind to the lesson you learn. You will never miss the goals.'

Self-Reflection

Sit in a quiet place, switch off your mobile, and take a few deep breaths to relax. Start a stopwatch and close your eyes. Imagine a digital clock in front of you with the number 24 in bright red colour.

Start counting down to zero. Watch that clock going 23, 22, 21, and so on.

Stop and start again from 24 if you are interrupted by any other thought or picture in your mind.

Record how much time it took for you to concentrate on the clock from 24 to 0 without interruption.

You probably will not be able to do it on your first attempt. So, don't worry. Keep at it, as you can only get better with time.

Where Is Your Attention?

As a mentor, one of the most rewarding experiences is helping clients achieve their goals. Rajneesh was a driven MBA student with a passion for entrepreneurship. However, he faced a common challenge that often hinders success in individuals—a lack of attention and focus.

We began our work by discussing the critical role that attention played in achieving success. We talked about the power of saying no, how distractions can derail even the most ambitious plans, and ways mindfulness can help regain control over attention. Rajneesh was receptive, and we began by tackling his tendency to multitask.

Once we addressed this issue, I introduced Rajneesh to mindfulness meditation. The practice of mindfulness helped him focus his attention on the present moment, allowing him to stay on track with his goals and avoid distractions. We started with short five-minute sessions and gradually increased the duration as he became more comfortable with the exercise.

The impact of mindfulness on Rajneesh was remarkable. He became more aware of his thoughts, emotions, and actions. Furthermore, he gained a newfound sense of clarity and purpose, which kept him motivated and engaged in his work. However, Rajneesh faced a significant challenge when it came to tackling his long-term goals. He was overwhelmed by the enormity of his aspirations, making it difficult to focus on the smaller steps needed to achieve them. Thus, we broke his long-term goals down into smaller, more achievable tasks. Here, I also advised him to perform a task with a complete focus for 20 minutes and then take a 5-minute break, repeating the process with the next hyperfocus slot of 20 minutes. This is called the Pomodoro Technique, which helped him gain a sense of progress and momentum, keeping him motivated and excited about his journey.

As we continued to work together, we identified and eliminated sources of distraction. Rajneesh was easily sidetracked by social media, so we worked on limiting his use during work hours. We also found him a quiet workspace and recommended noise-cancelling headphones to block out any potential interruptions.

Over time, I saw a significant transformation in Rajneesh. He was more focused and productive and was completing tasks with greater efficiency and accuracy. The positive effects of our work together spilled over into his personal life as well, where he found more balance and harmony.

Eventually, Rajneesh's hard work and dedication paid off, ability to focus and concentrate had become second nature to him. Despite the challenges of his entrepreneurial journey, his focus and concentration contributed significantly to his success. He launched his start-up with confidence and is well on his way to achieving all his goals and dreams.

Both focus and concentration are closely related terms. Focus is to know where the mind is and why it is there. Focus is the centre of attention—it can be an activity, person, or interest. Focus is a straight 'yes' or 'no' scenario. When we focus and say yes to one thing, we choose to give it our full attention. When we say yes to one thing, by default, we are saying no to several other things. Saying no is the first step to focusing well. Knowing what to say no to, when to say no, where to say no, and for how long should the no last (or not) can make a difference. Focus does not require you to permanently say no to other things. It's only about a particular moment. Say no to distractions now!

On the other hand, concentration is the degree or ability to give attention and maintain task performance without being disturbed by internal or external factors. For example, when people talk in a movie theatre, your concentration may shift for a moment, but the movie still remains in focus. Unlike focus, concentration isn't a simple yes or no. There are varying degrees of concentration depending on how focused you are in the moment. In today's world, we are constantly inattentive because diversions are just a click away—whether it's the latest news, Instagram, phone calls, WhatsApp, or other distractions.

Both success and failure depend solely on your ability to focus and concentrate, whether it's a project, fat-loss target, relationship goals, or anything else. The key is to realise that improving focus and concentration relies on external factors and some internalised behaviour.

Mantras to Unlock Sharpened Focus

1. Remove Distractions: Technology is the most significant source of distraction in our lives—phones, television, laptops, social media, e-mails, news, notifications, and much more. These apps and devices thrive on advertisements, and their focus is to divert your attention. You need to decide on your focus. Deleting these apps isn't a solution, but at the very least we can refrain from giving them control over us. Turn off your notifications, put your device on silent mode when focusing on a task, use earplugs while working, or keep your phone face down.
2. Keep the Distractions Away: Another effective method to focus completely is to make it difficult to reach the device. Ask someone to hide your phone while you work. The difficult it is to reach the device, the easier it is to focus.
3. Log Out: The effort of logging in each time will discourage the use. Do this for whatever distracts you the most. Delete unnecessary applications as doing so can reduce the number of notifications.
4. Minimise Multitasking: Multitasking is a myth! Doing multiple things simultaneously may feel productive, but it is counterproductive. It hampers focus, concentration, and quality of work, leaving you feeling burnt-out.

5. Sound Sleep: Lack of sound sleep also makes focus and concentration difficult. Ensure 6–8 hours of uninterrupted sleep every night.
6. Eat Balanced Meals: Avoid meals with a lot of sugar and carbohydrates, as they make you drowsy. Whereas, fibrous food keeps you active, so eat a lot of raw fruits and vegetables. Moreover, healthy fat also ensures proper functioning of the brain. So, eat nuts and berries. Lastly, keep your body hydrated.
7. Exercise: Body movement releases many hormones, such as endorphins and dopamine, that keep us happy and alert, thereby enhancing the power of memory and concentration.
8. Identify Your Focus Moments: Some of us can focus and concentrate well in the morning, whereas many others can only focus at nighttime. It's crucial to understand when you are the most attentive.
9. Take Short Breaks: Anything can get monotonous after a while, so when you start losing focus, take a quick break to regain it. Do whatever you like—take a walk, stretch, listen to music, or exercise.
10. Hyperfocus: This is a technique to train your brain to focus. Decide what you want to focus on, set the alarm for 20 minutes or more (but not over 30 minutes), and concentrate on that task. When the alarm goes off, take a 5-minute break to get up, and leave that room. Start again after the break.
11. Setup a Workspace: Instead of working anywhere and everywhere, assign yourself a place in the house as your designated focus area.

12. Set Priorities: Make a list of 25–50 things you want to achieve. Narrow down what you want to accomplish in a year. Then, narrow it down further to the goals you want to achieve in a month, week, or that day.
13. Meditation and Yoga: You can learn to train and tame the mind to be in the moment through regular meditation and yoga.

Focus and concentration are the superpowers that can transform your dreams into reality. Give your attention to evolve and they won't disappoint.

SUPERPOWER 30

MEMORY

Is Your Memory Prowess a Driving Force?

'Memories are like salt: the right amount brings out the flavour in food, too much ruins it.'

—Paulo Coelho

One day, looking at old pictures in my album, I started reminiscing about my past. I observed several preserved memories in these photo albums. I witnessed them all over again—my parents, childhood, school, time with friends, some kins, college, farewell party, my wedding, the birth of my daughters, deaths of loved ones, accidents, and honours.

I will turn 48 this year. With the addition of every new episode in my life, the memories of the past are starting to fade away. Many stories and memories started to play in my mind when I was going through the albums, leading to a tsunami of emotions. Some made me sad, others made me laugh; some made me blush, others turned me pale; some I was proud of, others I was embarrassed by; some were fierce, others were mild.

I enjoyed revisiting the photographs that were related to the happy moments, and I stayed with them for a while. However, I hurriedly turned the pages that were related to negative events that stirred sorrow in my heart. I wanted to destroy them as I equated my pain with a picture in the album. Tearing it down would incorrectly convey an end of my own pain—pain I feel even today.

My logical brain soon took over, 'Can I wipe off these memories from my mind? Can this purge be subjective and optional?'

I have wonderful memories that I want to keep for life. I would not have fared in academics if this memory power were not present. Even today, it is a boon.

But to hurt me, my brain also remembers to taunt me for being fat. I remember the insults and embarrassing moments that brought me down. I remember those whom I have not forgiven. For such occasions, memory is certainly a bane.

Our brain stores memories, both good and bad. Revisiting the good ones pleases us and returning to the bad ones causes us immense pain.

Self-Reflection

Write the memories from your past in your Evolve Journal and ensure you include both the good and the bad.

Memory Helps You Evolve

Memory is a superpower to remember things in detail. Our memories define us and are an integral part of us. While good memory power plays a significant role in success and happiness, it becomes weaker with age—sometimes because we are overloaded with information, confusing the brain about what to and what not to remember.

For instance, on a hectic day, you can note how it is harder to remember where you left the car keys or, at times, or you forget the names of familiar people. Sometimes, that word you want to say is on the tip of your tongue. You might miss an appointment because it slipped your mind.

Memory lapses can arise at any age, but the frequency may increase at an older age. However, like greying hair, memory loss is not a normal part of ageing. Yet, some changes in the brain can slow down your reflexes and cognitive responses, which is primarily due to the onset of other disorders.

Like physical health, your brain health can also be fostered by following certain healthy behaviours along with these research-based strategies and practices.

Mantras to Unlock the Power of Memory

1. Keep Learning: The brain is a muscle. Strong muscles mean good memory, and muscles improve by exercising. Learning new things is a good exercise for the brain, in turn, strengthening the memory. Step out of your comfort zone to learn anything new—learn to sing, dance, play an instrument, and paint. Exercise your brain and play challenging games like word puzzles and sudoku.
2. Use All Senses: While hearing, you are using only one sense, but it's crucial to use other senses as well. Speak what you hear, write it down, and then repeat it without looking at the note. In this manner, you will be using your ear (listening), tongue (speaking), eyes (reading), and skin (writing).

3. Use Acronyms, Abbreviations, and Mnemonics: This is a time-tested way of memorising things. Remember how you used VIBGYOR to remember the colour spectrum? Or 'King Henry Died Mother Didn't Cry Much' to remember the units of measurement? Apply the same method to learning new things and skills.
4. Group the Information: Divide the data into manageable parts, like remembering a 10-digit phone number becomes easier when grouped in two or three manageable chunks (94251-49369 or 9425-149-369).
5. Be Organised: Economise the use of memory and assign a specific place to the regular items. When you organise your belongings, you do not need to remember a lot of unnecessary information, such as 'Where are my keys?' because the mind knows the keys are on the key holder in the entryway.
6. Make a To-Do List: A to-do list is handy for enhancing several superpowers—memory is one of them.
7. Holistic Wellness: Eat healthy, stay hydrated, exercise regularly, sleep well, and meditate. These five elements play certain roles in sharpening and maintaining memory power. Avoid excessive salt and sugar, fried food, oil, butter, cheese, and red meat; take them only in moderation or, if possible, completely avoid.
8. Maintain a Sleep Schedule: Irregular and disturbed sleep pattern can cause memory loss. Thus, it is essential to maintain a regular sleep schedule.
9. Avoid Devices before Sleeping: Keep all the bright lights away—mobile, laptops, and television—an hour before your bedtime. These devices emit blue light that disturbs one's sleep cycle. And as mentioned in the previous point,

without enough sound sleep, the brain gets easily tired and loses its power.

10. Stay Active: Move your body, walk, or exercise regularly. Yoga needs a special mention here as it has a far-reaching impact on memory. Shedding extra fat also helps in improving memory.
11. Meditate Regularly: Meditation has a proven impact on memory, learning, and mindfulness. Walking in serene surroundings is also a form of meditation. Find your style and frequently practice it.
12. Socialise: People who socialise often experience slower memory decline compared to those who do not.
13. Consume Caffeine and Alcohol: According to an article in Harvard Health Publishing, both caffeine and alcohol positivcly impact memory power. Both should be consumed in moderation and avoided before sleep as they can disturb your sleep cycle.
14. Use Your Non-dominant Hand: You can try using your non-dominant hand for harmless jobs. This can keep your brain active and memory power strong. It also helps in stimulating the other side of the brain, making both sides work in harmony. The more, the merrier!

After talking about sharpening the memory, the next important thing is to stay away from those bad memories and focusing on safeguarding your brain health. To relieve the pain of old, unhappy memories, take a reality check by asking yourself, 'Can I help this?' Don't scratch old wounds, keep yourself busy, be calm, and stay positive. Include some chosen rituals and practices in your daily routine to make it a habit. Keep your mind open to learning and keep at it.

SUPERPOWER 31

SELF-REGULATION

Do Your Emotions Control You?

'There are always two forces working against each other within us.'

—Paramahansa Yogananda

I am a cautious driver. I am a follower of rules. Even at midnight, I stop at the signal, although my not-so-metro town roads are mostly empty at night. Frankly, I get livid when others do not follow the rules.

One day, I was late for a lunch meeting. The traffic was thin, and the signal turned red. I stopped, and a few more vehicles halted as well. The man driving a luxury car behind me started honking as soon as the signal turned green. The man driving the luxury car was well dressed and probably well-educated. That day was not a usual day. Unlike my usual, calm self, I rolled down my window and yelled at him.

The guy raced his luxury car, rolled down the window, and gave me a charming smile. Just a smile! His smile made me awkward, and I started thinking, 'Why did this happen? How can some random guy influence my behaviour? Why am I not able to exercise self-control?'

Later that day, I reflected on this episode with a relaxed mind, and I came to the realisation that I was losing control. It was then that I decided to start practising meditation, which has since immensely helped me. I no longer find myself getting offended easily and have gained better control and regulation of my emotions and reactions.

Self-Reflection

Reflect in your Evolve Journal on how you react in traffic. Is it challenging to regulate your reactions in emotional, stressful, or demanding situation, such as when stuck in heavy traffic? How comfortable are you with resisting temptations like looking at your mobile phone or eating junk food? Can you maintain regularity in your actions by waking up early or exercising frequently?\

Regulating Your Emotions

Self-regulation is a superpower to control emotions rather than letting them control your thoughts and behaviour. It is a superpower to regulate what you feel and do. It is mainly concerned with discipline, following a routine, controlling appetite as well as emotions. It is the ability to keep troublesome emotions in check, maintain control over impulses, think before acting. Self-regulation also comprises the ability to bounce back from distress, manage emotional tsunamis, and act consistently with your values.

Self-regulation relates to behaviour, which involves taking action in your best interest, even when you don't feel like doing so. When you don't want to wake up early or don't feel like going to the office but choose to act otherwise, you are exercising behavioural self-regulation.

Emotional self-regulation deals with regulating and controlling strong emotions like sadness and anger. When you talk to yourself to calm down your intense emotions or pull yourself out of a bad mood, you display effective emotional self-regulation.

According to psychologist Stuart Shanker, 'Self-control is about inhibiting strong impulses; self-regulation [is about] reducing the frequency and intensity of strong impulses by managing stress-load and recovery. In fact, self-regulation is what makes self-control possible, or, in many cases, unnecessary.'

Although self-regulation is considered more critical for children and adolescents, it develops automatically during their formative years. Yet, its importance cannot be ignored for adults because conscious effort and consistent practise can help change things. Adults with self-regulation capabilities can navigate their professional and familial lives more easily. They can keep themselves from yelling in the workplace or picking a fight at the roadside. People with better self-regulation mostly outperform less regulated adults—both personally and professionally.

Mantras to Unlock Better Self-Regulation

1. Cultivate Mindfulness: Learn to live in the moment. When you are aware of the present and not thinking about the past or the future, you are better positioned to look at thoughts, feelings, and behaviours without judgment. Your ability to make conscious decisions enhances.
2. Interrupt Negative Thoughts: Learn to challenge your thoughts and replace them with positive ones. Reframe

inner dialogues and thoughts to encourage better reactions to situations.

3. Notice Emotions: Knowing your emotions is the first step to regulating and controlling them. Seek an understanding of why you feel what you feel. Knowing can help identify and understand yours as well as others' feelings. Once you are aware of the 'what' and 'why' of your emotions, you can then choose how to resolve them.
4. Identify Triggers: What are your stressors or triggers that cause uncomfortable emotions? Knowing your triggers will timely anticipate your emotions, leading you to use coping skills as and when needed. For instance, I ditch my diet whenever I pass by a Domino's outlet while feeling hungry. The trigger here is hunger, not the Domino's outlet. Once I became aware of this, I started carrying healthy snacks in my car to regulate my dietary habits.
5. Slow Down Your Thinking: Thinking before reacting can help with self-regulation. Calm your mind and relax before responding to any situation. Consider what can happen if you follow your emotions.
6. Observe Your Body: Your body provides signals, such as a racing heart, excessive sweating, itching, etc. Be aware of those before identifying and monitoring the physical changes.
7. Live with Integrity: Be a role model, practise what you preach, create trusting environments, and live with your values.
8. Set a Daily Routine: Commit yourself to a routine. Take the initiative and stay persistent in working towards your routine and goals even when it's the last thing you feel like doing.

9. Relax When Upset: Keep calm by removing yourself from the stressful situation. Exercise relaxation practices, such as deep breathing, progressive relaxation, taking a walk, or any else that works for you.
10. Mind Your Company: Believe in your abilities and surround yourself with positive and supportive people.
11. Celebrate Success: Pat yourself on the back when you successfully self-resist an indulgence. Keep your trusted friends and family in the loop so that they can also congratulate and motivate you on your successful attempts.
12. Manage Your Time: Set your goals or targets for the day. Schedule and budget your time for them, so you don't need to rush to accomplish too much at a time. Establish a routine, a regular time, and a place for most of your activities. Follow some rituals that can make sticking to a routine more manageable. For example, you can prepare a healthy breakfast at night to avoid grabbing an unhealthy snack on the go.

When you learn some balancing acts to suit your temperament, you easily self-regulate your habits, thoughts, emotions, behaviours, and reactions. When you practise these balancing acts, they become a way of life.

SUPERPOWER
32

CONSISTENCY

Unravel Your Prospects

'Consistency of performance is essential. You don't have to be exceptional every week but as a minimum you need to be at a level that even on a bad day you get points on the board.'

—Sean Dyche

An aspiring singer was being trained by a much-disciplined master. Practising the same stanza became a quotidian affair without going any further. One day, out of frustration, the singer ran off and decided to quit singing. The next day, a singing competition was organised at the restaurant where she went to dine. She thought of taking a chance. But the only song she could think of at that time was the same passage she had been practising for months, and she sang.

Her outstanding performance left everyone spellbound, including the judges. The judges praised her, felicitated her, and asked who her mentor was. It was only then that she realised the intention of her mentor. The girl was none other than the famous Japanese singer, Fubuki Koshiji.

Self-Reflection

Reflect on your consistency. What factors motivate you or rob you of your consistency? Make a note of the specifics in your Evolve Journal.

Consistency Is the Key

We all have goals, and we make plans to achieve them as well. Some of us even take the first step but withdraw soon after. Very few have the courage and confidence to keep moving. Although we know that the tortoise's perseverance made it win the race, most of us quit after a while. Does it sound familiar to you?

Whatever you want and whatever you are looking to achieve—big or small, professional or personal—consistency is the key to all things in life. According to the Oxford Dictionary, consistency is defined as the quality of always behaving in the same way or always having the same opinions, standards, etc.

Consistency means adhering to your principles, focusing on the behaviour and necessary actions to achieve your goal and sticking to them, and repetitively doing them. When you keep moving towards the goal, you get closer to it. Consistency is the make or break when you are clear about your goals and confident about the approach.

Consistency is based on patience, belief, and value. When you want to see tangible progress too soon, you might invite inconsistencies. One needs patience to be consistent. Consistency is lost when you are suspicious about whether what you are doing is correct. One must have a belief in the approach. We also fail at being consistent when we do not see the value from the returns when the result is insignificant. Consistency occurs when we are patient, trust the process, and see value in it.

Consistency is significant in creating habits. Doing anything consistently for 21 days makes it a habit. However, habits can change. So, stretch yourself further to make it your lifestyle. When you maintain this habit for another 90 days, it becomes your lifestyle, your default setting, which is rock solid.

Your consistency in this Evolve Journey is the key to becoming a better you. Do the daily exercises and practices consciously for just 21 days, then maintain the flow for 90 days to make them your default setting. They will come naturally, with no conscious effort.

Mantras to Unlock Consistency

1. Start with One Non-negotiable: We always want more and strive for consistency in many areas, but achieving this isn't impossible. However, begin with just one non-negotiable. For instance, if your goal is to achieve a fit body, smaller goals such as maintaining a healthy diet and engaging in regular exercise could be considered. Choose one to start with. Once you begin to see results in that chosen area, you can then add the next one.
2. Morning Rituals: Make it your morning ritual for it to become a part of your daily flow.
3. Make it a Habit: Pull your socks up for 21 days, even if you don't feel like doing it.
4. Set Reminders: We tend to forget about things that are out of our sight. We neither see them nor hear them. Here,

setting up reminders can help. Whenever you set goals for yourself, commit to yourself. Say it aloud. Repeat!

Set up reminders in your visible surroundings. Strategically place sticky notes on the mirror, fridge, dashboard, work desk, etc. If the reminder is about healthy eating, place it on your snack shelf or refrigerator. If it's about a career goal, then place it on your work desk. A reminder note on the mirror is a good option if the goal is about weight loss. Your mobile and laptop screensavers and backgrounds are also good choices.

Setting up a vision board is another great option. Create a vision board, write down your goals and place pictures. After all, a picture is worth a thousand words.

Lastly, the easiest way to remind yourself is by setting an alarm.

5. Get an Accountability Partner: Ask someone to make you accountable for your progress by asking and keeping a record. It can be anyone—a family member, your friends, or a colleague. You can also do things together—both acting as accountability partners for each other.
6. Reward Yourself: Gratification keeps us motivated. So, reward yourself for achieving even a small target. Make sure to celebrate small wins.
7. Break Down Big Goals: Big goals and longer durations are overwhelming. Split the big goal into stages and phases. For example, the significant 20 kg weight loss in 1 year can be split into 1 kg every week or 3 kg every month.
8. Add Value: We lose interest if the value we perceive does not excite us. Goals that are easy and too small for us to achieve do not challenge us. Our brain thinks it to be easy, and can be completed in no time, so why do it now?

Therefore, you should set goals that are a bit difficult to achieve. Such as, if you think 20 push-ups a day is child's play, set your goal to 30. The trick is to let your goal attract you by adding more value and perspective. Remember, it works like compound interest. These small goals will finally lead to achieving bigger ones.

9. Minimise Distractions: It is challenging to be consistent when there are distractions around us.
10. Forgive Failure: Humans are bound to be inconsistent at times. We get tired and slip some days. All of us can be inconsistent at times, and that's okay. Just ensure that you get back on track before the flow breaks.

Being consistent is a long-term game. Don't be lazy. Stay consistent. Remember, miracles may get you there but only consistency can keep you there.

SUPERPOWER 33

DISCIPLINE

What Is Your Default?

'Continuous improvement is better than delayed perfection.'

—Mark Twain

One day, two ants came across two giant cookies. 'Wow, look at the size of these cookies,' said the first ant. 'Just one can feed my whole family for months.'

The second ant asked, 'But how will we take these big cookies home? We are so tiny.'

'It is tough, but let's give it a go,' said the first one and started pushing the cookie back and forth. Suddenly, a tiny piece of the cookie broke off.

'Yahoo! I am taking this piece home,' the first ant exclaimed.

The second ant was not confident about the idea, and said, 'Do whatever you want. I'm not part of this. I don't approve of wasting energy and time on this little piece. I will only take the whole cookie back to my family.'

So, the first ant took the small piece home and quickly returned. The second ant was still making unsuccessful efforts pulling and pushing the cookie. The first ant broke off another small portion of the cookie and took it home. This exercise of breaking and taking a small piece home went on for an entire day, and even a few other ants joined in. They kept at it until the whole cookie moved.

The second ant, still struggling to move the giant cookie, got tired and gave up. She went home empty-handed.

Self-Reflection

Reflect on your life and in your Evolve Journal write down the five habits you are struggling to make or break.

Make or Break Habits

I asked trainees, during a 'make or break habits' workshop, why and when they switched their goalposts. The answers were usually, 'When I get bored,' 'Because I hate hard work,' and 'When I don't see the results.'

Does this sound familiar?

Driven by motivation, you start towards your new goal and work hard every day on your newly discovered passion. Then you miss one day, then you miss it here, and you miss it there. Finally, you realise your motivation is gone, your passion has disappeared, and you have missed the bus. You then discover a new passion, and this cycle begins again.

I do not know about you, but it has happened to me many a time. We know that being disciplined is essential and that it is the one thing that helps us achieve our goals, yet we stumble. We are consistent about setting up new plans, bursting with energy, stopping before the finish line, and beating ourselves up. We are consistent at failing to be consistent and disciplined.

The good news is that half the battle is won when you understand why you fail at discipline. Most people fail when they focus on the final result because they don't see the everyday progress. The result does not feel significant and we lose motivation and fail to be disciplined.

I was obese. I weighed 70 kg at the age of 17. I had resolved a million times to lose weight. I wanted to weigh 60 kg. I wanted to look and feel beautiful. Every time I started my weight-loss journey, I was so absorbed with losing the 10 kg that I overlooked whether I reached my goal of 1kg per week. I was still making progress, but instead of motivating myself by celebrating small milestones, I focused on how far I still was from my dream weight.

Another common reason to fail at discipline is hard work. People get overwhelmed because of working hard. Contemplating about practising and doing anything for hours every day, over several weeks, months, or years, overwhelms us because we often confuse discipline with intensity.

I made plans to lose weight—no junk food, a lot of raw vegetables and fruits, working out every day for an hour, walking 10,000 steps, drinking 4–5 litres of water, and seven hours of a good night's sleep. Now, doesn't it sound overwhelming? It's definitely a lot to achieve each day! Discipline becomes difficult when we seek an all-or-nothing approach. You don't need to start with everything all at once. The key is to start slow, with a few initial changes, and add more when you get used to the previous ones. For instance, I started with drinking 3 litres of water every day for a week, I then added another litre, then another after a week. From a completely sedentary lifestyle to 10,000 steps is a huge task. So, I started with 2,000 steps to begin with and gradually added more when I was comfortable with the previous goal. It's okay if you miss reaching your daily target sometimes; just make sure to do it every day. Discipline, not intensity, is the word.

It was my 38th birthday, and I weighed 92 kg. This was when I finally resolved to shed those extra kilos after considering 'why was I not consistent?' The answer was discipline. I lost 35 kg in 18 months and am still maintaining my ideal weight. I now weigh 62 kg at the age of 48.

Let's dive deeper into how to cultivate everyday discipline in life to make or break certain habits.

Mantras to Attain Discipline

1. Mark Your Goals: I know there are several things you want to become disciplined with, but decide on the one thing you want most and tackle it first. Now, don't overwhelm your mind with an all-or-nothing approach; start small. If you want to develop ten good habits, don't start with all ten on your list. Prioritise them and approach them one at a time.
2. Refine the 'Why': Your why could be significant or small, but it should be *your* why. Ask yourself if it is personal. Do you relate to this? Refine your why. An unclear and shallow reason is not enough to motivate you every day. Dig deeper and be specific.
3. Stick to a Schedule: When you know in advance what is to be done and when it is to be done, it encourages discipline. Make a to-do list, use a planner, or set reminders on your phone. Follow what suits you. When you schedule your day, you have clarity on your time, stopping you from over-committing. This helps maintain discipline.

4. Anticipate a Dip: The world is not perfect, nor is our discipline. We have experienced that life is not a smooth road, and it always is a series of rises and falls. We get disciplined, and we do things for days, which eventually shows results. But, when we suddenly fail, we also fail in our discipline and don't see the results. A dip is normal after some success. Anticipate it. Determine in advance what you will do during a fall. Always have a Plan B!
5. Avoid Obsession with Quality: Focus on developing a rhythm. Do it even when you don't feel like doing it, even when you are uninspired and unmotivated. Don't obsess about the quality, just keep at it until you find the rhythm. When you don't feel like working out, don't workout, but make sure to follow the routine—of getting up, getting dressed, and instead of working out just stretch or go for a walk. Remember: Consistency, not intensity.
6. Establish Accountability: Find yourself an accountability partner who can question you and remind you of your goals. This partner can be any trusted friend or family member. You can also establish accountability by announcing your plans to a larger audience, like your colleagues or your social media following. They may not actually ask you about your daily progress, but this declaration alone will naturally generate accountability.
7. Forgive Yourself: Getting tired and sometimes failing at discipline is inevitable. Don't beat yourself up for not doing it. Forgive yourself and move on. That's the only choice you have.
8. Don't Rely on Motivation: Motivation can get you there, but it is only habit (Clear 2018) that keeps you there. You cannot stay motivated forever. Motivation will leave you

someday, but habits die hard. Make it your habit in 21 days and your lifestyle in 90 days. Create discipline and make things happen in autopilot mode, even without motivation.

When you find your way to become disciplined, you become more dependable, predictable, and comforting to be with. Discipline is a practice; it will strengthen over time. Discipline is a work-in-progress; keep adding it to new areas of your life. Remember, discipline is not about quality and perfection but about showing up each day.

SUPERPOWER
34

PHYSICAL WELLNESS

Is Your Body in Harmony?

'Health is a state of body. Wellness is a state of being.'

—J. Stanford

An affluent man was concerned about his carelessness. He used to lose his pens every so often. He asked many for advice, but nothing helped. One day, he met his childhood friend, who suggested that he buy the most expensive pen he could afford.

Although the man was not sure about the idea, he agreed and bought a 22-carat Cross Gold pen. After around six months, when they met again, his friend asked if he still had the pen.

The man said, 'Surprisingly, now I have become more careful about the pen, and I still have this 22-carat Cross Gold pen.‘

His friend said that he was not careless; it was the value of the pen that stopped him from misplacing it. The value of the pen made all the difference. We care for the things we value the most.

The friend who suggested this resolution was J. R. D. Tata.

Self-Reflection

Reflect on your daily habits and routines, and answer these simple questions: Do you wake up full of energy or are you often distracted by issues related to your body, such as pain, headaches, discomfort, and fatigue? Do you feel optimistic about the day ahead and confident that you can handle whatever comes your way? Do you struggle to complete tasks during the day because you feel tired or experience a lack of energy and enthusiasm? Do you value your wellness?

The Pursuit of Physical Wellness

Imagine that you are a CEO of a company. You can shape the company's destiny by setting its goals, targets, and values. It's an immense responsibility, isn't it?

Now, this company is You Pvt. Ltd., and it aims for life satisfaction and wellness. Life satisfaction refers to the overall contentment a person feels with their life, encompassing various facets such as mood, relationships, achievements, self-concept, and coping abilities. Wellness extends beyond physical health, encompassing dimensions like intellectual, emotional, social, spiritual, vocational, financial, and environmental well-being.

As CEO, your decisions and actions drive the pursuit of wellness. Physical wellness, in particular, is foundational, as it underpins other aspects of well-being. Without physical wellness, optimal engagement in life is hindered. Recognise the interconnectedness of wellness dimensions, with physical wellness as the common thread. Without physical wellness, one cannot achieve mental well-being. Lack of physical compatibility and illness may trigger mental conditions, such as stress, depression, anxiety, etc. These conditions may further impact cognitive abilities, hampering learning skills. Difficulty in learning will then influence intellectual and vocational well-being. Not performing well at work and an unhealthy mood and attitude will impact relationships and careers. Together, all this will eventually affect your financial wellness. Thus, physical wellness should never be ignored to become a good CEO of You Pvt. Ltd.

Physical wellness comprises more than just disease prevention and body weight. It involves cultivating healthy habits across dimensions like nutrition, hydration, sleep, exercise, relaxation, hygiene, meditation, and social connectedness.

Regardless of age, occupation, or health status, prioritising physical wellness is key to thriving. While some conditions may be irreversible, their progression can be slowed through physical wellness practices. It is a matter of choice and action we take to achieve the goal of You Pvt. Ltd. CEOs who make thoughtful investments in physical wellness every day thrive for life, come what may.

The first step to physical wellness is checking your body weight and composition. Once you know which areas need more focus, it becomes easier to manage. Then, start following practices and exercises to manage your physical wellness. While following any of the suggestions below, please be mindful of your allergies, infections, and other medical conditions. To be a successful CEO of your company, take baby steps and start with small, conscious changes in every dimension. The exercises and practices suggested below should apply to anybody and everybody, but here is a disclaimer: *The tools suggested below are not exhaustive. The human body is magnificent, and each body is different; hence, be mindful of the steps that may not apply to you, and listen to your doctor.*

Mantras to Unlock the Power of Mindful Nutrition

Food fuels our bodies. Be mindful of the quality of food you consume. Also, take care of how and what you fuel your body with:

1. Eat Raw: Adding more wholesome ingredients to your plate, such as salads, fruits, sprouts, nuts, berries, and much more. Eat as much raw food as you can. Furthermore, avoid overcooking cereals, pulses, and vegetables.
2. Eat Fresh: Avoid processed and packaged foods. Fresh, homemade food is any day better than what's been processed in a factory.
3. Carry Healthy Snacks: To avoid fast-food and roadside eateries, carry your food and drinks whenever you're on the road. Keep some munchies handy with you—an apple or any other fruit, raw veggies, dry fruits, a home-cooked meal, fresh fruit juice, or buttermilk.
4. Chew Well: As it's said, eat your water and drink your food. Chew your food so well that you don't swallow it but drink it. Eat not only with your tongue but with the other senses as well—your eyes, nose, feelings, and mind. Watch what you eat. Think about how what you're eating will influence your overall health.
5. Be Mindful: When you eat, only eat. Don't eat in front of the television, don't use mobile phones, and don't read newspapers or books while eating. Avoid multitasking,

as when we do so, our mind gets confused, and we end up overeating. Eating mindfully, with all your senses, can improve the satisfaction you receive from the food.

6. Eat the Rainbow: Include five (out of seven) colours in your daily diet—red, yellow, orange, green, blue, purple, and white. Including all five colours will fulfil your daily requirements for all the necessary nutrients. Some examples: Red-coloured foods—tomato, apple, pomegranate, bell pepper, kidney beans, strawberries, radish, beetroot, etc. Yellow- and orange-coloured foods—pumpkin, orange, lemon, papaya, bell pepper, yellow dal, mango, melon, pineapple, peach, etc. Green-coloured foods—all leafy vegetables, green pulses and beans, peas, avocado, kiwi, green apple, etc. Blue- and purple-coloured foods—eggplant (brinjal), purple cabbage, purple carrots, black olives, blueberries, blackberries, purple grapes, purple plums, prunes, passionfruit, dark cherries, etc. Brown-coloured foods—wheat and most grains, onions, garlic, cauliflower, lychee, banana, milk and milk products, etc.
7. Eat Regional and Seasonal: Nature has intelligently designed everything. Regional and seasonal food is always loaded with the nutrients required in that region and season. Eat local and seasonal to stay healthy.

Mantras to Unlock the Power of Mindful Hydration

60 per cent of our body is made of water. It is responsible for maintaining our body temperature, metabolising food, regulating hunger, keeping electrolytes in balance, lubricating joints, producing saliva, and flushing out body waste. We also

constantly lose water through sweat, urine, and breath. Thus, keeping the body hydrated throughout the day is crucial for proper functioning. To determine how much water is sufficient for you, use this simple formula: Divide your body weight by 20, as our body requires one litre of water for every 20 kg.

1. Eat Your Water: Sip, don't gulp your water and other fluids. Start your day with water by drinking a glass right after waking up.
2. Be Regular: Don't wait till you feel thirsty. Spread out your daily requirements throughout the day.
3. Drink Small Amounts: Don't drink too much water at a time because your body will flush out the excess soon.
4. Drink before Meals: This will prevent overeating and lubricate the passage beforehand for food to travel easily.
5. Carry a Water Bottle: Invest in a sturdy bottle and carry it wherever you go.
6. Be Mindful: Drink more fluids in hot weather and when you are active. Recognise your body's signals. People often confuse thirst with hunger.
7. Add Flavour: If you find plain water boring, add calorie-free flavouring to your water. You can experiment with Tulsi leaves, lemon slices, or any other fruits or vegetables to infuse your water.
8. Consume Water-Rich Fruits and Vegetables: Not only water, but the body also hydrates through food.
9. LimitCaffeine: Beverages like tea, coffee, soda, sports drinks, etc., can carry high amounts of caffeine, in turn, making you dehydrated.

Mantras to Unlock the Power of Sound Sleep

An average adult requires a minimum of 6–8 hours of sound sleep daily. It is essential to follow good sleep hygiene.

1. Set a Routine: Not only a sleep routine but follow a routine in general. Avoid caffeine, nicotine, and alcohol about 4–6 hours before going to bed.
2. Develop Your Sleep Ritual: Create habits like brushing your teeth, changing to your nightwear, writing in a journal, meditating, deep breathing, etc. Involve yourself in some quiet and calm activities before going to bed.
3. Sleep When Sleepy: Don't spend too much time awake in bed. Go to bed only when you feel sleepy. If you cannot fall asleep even after 20 minutes of lying in bed, get up and engage in some calming or boring activities. Some people like to read before bed as it helps them sleep.
4. Avoid Bright Lights: Stop using all your devices at least an hour before going to bed. The bed is only for sleeping. Ensure exposure to sunlight during the day for a good night's sleep.
5. Avoid Naps: If you struggle to get a good night's sleep, avoid taking naps. However, if you cannot do without it, make sure you do not nap for over 20–30 minutes.
6. Eat Right: As mentioned above, eating a healthy and balanced diet helps in promoting sleep. However, the timing of your meal consumption is also crucial. Some people find it difficult to sleep on an empty stomach; if you are one of them, have some light snacks before bed. But remember not to have anything heavy before bedtime, as it interrupts sleep.

7. Create Comfortable Space: Make sure the environment of your room is as per your preference. Generally, the main concerns are temperature, light, linens, mattress, and noise. Avoid extreme heat or cold. The best option is to sleep in a quiet, dark, and cool room with sufficient cover to keep you warm. Use curtains, eye masks, and earplugs to prevent unwanted lights and sounds. If you prefer, you may keep the night lights on.
8. Sleep Diary. If you face sleep problems even after following the above-mentioned mantras, consider keeping a sleep diary. This can help you determine what works for you and what does not. Make a sleep record for two weeks—note down what time you sleep, what time you get up, how long you were awake in bed, what you were doing when you were awake, total sleep time, and other details related to your sleep patterns. You can also use a smartwatch to monitor night sleep.

Don't ignore your medical conditions. Follow these tips and tricks simultaneously with prescriptions by your physician, if any.

Mantras to Unlock the Power of Mindful Exercise

In today's world, our lives are distressed by sedentary lifestyles along with changing food habits and dietary patterns. This has increased the significance of regular exercising. Exercising can improve mood and promote a sense of well-being. Regular exercise also improves and maintains the ability of our body to perform daily activities efficiently, at all ages and stages of life.

1. Workout Regularly: Regular exercise is essential for physical well-being, overall endurance, strength, balance, and flexibility. Endurance activities like brisk walking, swimming, and cycling improve cardiovascular health, while strength training enhances muscle function for daily tasks. Balance exercises, such as yoga and stability training, prevent falls and support mobility. Flexibility exercises maintain joint health and range of motion, promoting overall physical well-being.
2. Make Small Changes: Minor changes in your daily routine can also help in increasing endurance. For instance, take the stairs instead of the elevator.
3. Warm Up and Cool Down: Never forget to warm up and cool down the body with gentle movements before and after any exercise.
4. Listen to Your Body: Be mindful of the changes and movements in your body. Exercise should not cause dizziness, chest pain, or heartburn. Stop immediately if you feel uneasy.
5. Stay Hydrated: The body dehydrates while working out. Ensure you drink adequate liquids before, after, and during the exercises.
6. Breath: Be mindful of your breathing, and consciously inhale and exhale while performing any exercise. Don't hold your breath.
7. Support: Take the support of a chair or a wall for balancing exercises until you feel confident.
8. Be Patient: It takes time to regain strength, endurance, balance, and flexibility. Don't expect too much too soon. Be patient and exercise to the point that is comfortable for you.

Your range of motion will automatically improve after a few repetitions. Increase the intensity when you feel comfortable and confident in your abilities. Just be consistent.

Talk to an expert when you are unsure about any particular exercise. Consult your physician when you start a new workout regimen.

MANTRAS TO UNLOCK THE POWER OF MINDFUL RELAXATION

We often confuse relaxing with sitting ideally, doing nothing, or simply sleeping. However, when you are not mindful, you don't receive the full advantage of relaxation. I believe fasting, which is integral to Indian traditions, is the best means of relaxation. *Langhanam param aushadham* is an ancient Sanskrit saying which means, 'Fasting is the supreme medicine.'

Fasting is a superpower that empowers the body, mind, and soul. It can be explained as mindful moderation, either total withdrawal or reduction, from a certain activity or thing for a specific period. One consciously decides not to do something and gives some organs a rest while they fast. I would recommend embracing six types of fasting to achieve holistic wellness.

1. Fasting of Food: It gives the digestive system a much-needed rest. This fast can be customised to suit individual abilities, medical conditions, and physical requirements. Fast with only water, only liquids—water and other non-alcoholic liquids like milk, juices, etc.—or only fruits and vegetables. Anything you have during this time should not be cooked or processed in any form—no spices, salt, or sugar. Only food in its natural form is allowed. This type of

fasting is recommended once a week. You can also practise intermittent fasting every day.

2. Fasting of Speech: Practise *maun* (speechlessness) for 24 hours of the chosen day. On other days of the month, be mindful of what you speak and practice true speech—don't tell lies, don't speak in a harmful or hurtful manner, or don't be pessimistic in your speech. Speech fasting can offer insight and improved focus.
3. Fasting of Breath: You can be more mindful when you are conscious of your breath. Breath fasting is about slowing the pace of your breath and being aware of your breathing. Inhale slowly and exhale at an even slower pace. You can also practise holding your breath after you inhale and exhale every time. Breathe fasting is effective in reducing stress and fatigue. It can be observed every day for 15–30 minutes.
4. Fasting of Movement: This fast is for restricting body movements and staying still for some time. This does not include sleeping or lying down while watching television; it is mindful stillness. Close your eyes. Sit still with an erect spine. Hands close to your body, palms facing down on your thighs, and both feet touching the ground. Be mindful of your breath or any other rhythmic sound. This fast can be observed anytime you feel restless. Stillness achieved even for a minute or two can give wonderful results. This fast is often clubbed with breath fasting. This fast can also be observed daily in one sitting for at least 15 minutes.
5. Fasting of Thoughts: The most difficult of all fasts is the fasting of thoughts. Thoughtlessness requires immense practise, even for a minute, because 20–40 thoughts pop up in our minds every second. The yogic practice of meditation

is a time-tested approach to attaining mindfulness. This fast should be observed daily for a duration that is viable for you.

Mantras to Unlock the Power of Meditation

Meditation benefits both body and mind. It helps improve focus and changes the brain. Reflect on your present state of mind and consider what and how you feel. Meditation makes you aware of your surroundings without getting overwhelmed. It gives you control over your reactions. Meditation helps develop an awareness of the present moment, where we can create space for ourselves—space to breathe and space to think about ourselves and our actions and reactions. Meditation will give you better control of You Pvt. Ltd. (Harari 2018). There are several ways to meditate. You can explore where you belong and what comes easy and naturally to you.

1. No Need of Gear: You require nothing to practice meditation—only yourself, time, and effort.
2. Connect with the Self: No, there will be no communication with the supreme power. The purpose of meditation is awareness and being in the moment. Pay attention to the present moment, your feelings, and your thoughts without judging yourself or others.
3. Mind Will Wander: Although the goal is to achieve thoughtlessness, don't resist too hard. The mind will try to stay anywhere and everywhere but where you are. So, consciously bring your mind back to the present moment when you realise that it has drifted to something or somewhere else.

4. Avoid Judgement: Many questions will arise in your mind when you sit and meditate. Let the thoughts come and go. Don't judge yourself for your thoughts.
5. Follow a Routine: Fix a time of the day to meditate. Early morning or before bed is a good choice, but you can do it at any fixed time as per your preference.
6. Be Still: Sit in a calm and quiet place. Be still, close your eyes, and feel the moment. You can sit in any position you find comfortable—on a chair, on the floor in Dhyana Mudra, kneeling, and even on the bed. Just remember that you need to stay still. I would suggest avoiding sitting on the bed in the beginning. Once you have learnt how to meditate, do it wherever you wish.
7. Set a Time Limit: For a beginner, even five minutes is enough. Set a timer for five minutes, and after the timer goes off, reflect on your experience. When did you realise that you drifted from the moment? How many times during those five minutes did you drift? What thoughts and feelings caused the drift?
8. Raise the Bar: Once you successfully meditate for five minutes, keep increasing the time. Do it for 10, 15, or up to 30 minutes every day.
9. Practise Is the Key: The mind will wander, and self-criticism will arise, but the key is to realise that you are stuck somewhere else, and you are not in the moment. Try to consciously get back to the moment. Go away, come back, and be kind to yourself.

Mantras to Unlock the Power of Social Connectedness

Connection is a subjective expression that shows feeling close to someone and a sense of belongingness. Staying connected with family and friends can improve both physical and mental well-being.

1. Socialise: Meet people and spend time with them. Attend community events and participate in activities that interest you. Step out of your house for a walk, run, or cycle, and meet people. Get out of your head, talk to people, and greet them even if you don't know them. Be proactive. Take time to call or meet people you've been thinking about.
2. Be Optimistic: People don't like the company of those who talk negatively. Always have something good to say.
3. Social Support: This is the availability of help and support to an individual from your social network. This support can be both provided and received. It can be the feelings of love, care, sympathy, empathy, motivation, and much more. Or it can be physical. Social support can be improved by sharing, helping, and supporting others when they are in need. When you need support, ask for help. Stay close to your inner circle. When you are closely connected, speak regularly, and be emotionally available.
4. Sense of Belonging: The feeling of being connected, wanted, and valued by others is the sense of belongingness. It is the opposite of loneliness. Being desired by others and a sense of belongingness to class, category, groups, family, or friends that is greater than themselves is an inherent desire of all human beings. A higher sense of belongingness can

be achieved by being friendly to people. Be present when people want to talk.

5. Spend Quality Time: Nourish relationships with love, care, time, and support. Regularly spend quality time with loved ones.

Physical wellness is being aware of the changes and requirements of the body at various ages and stages of life and taking care of them for holistic well-being. Keeping your body healthy and happy will help you get through everyday stress, make you stronger, and aid in living a better life.

SUPERPOWER 35

FINANCIAL WELLNESS

Do You Have a Financial Plan?

'A person can be highly educated, professionally successful, and financially illiterate.'

—Robert Kiyosaki

Somnath and Sunil were both 28 when they joined BHEL Ltd. in 2008. As BHEL was India's largest public sector company, it was a dream come true for both of them. They were earning well, enjoying the perks of the public-sector job, and planning their future.

Sunil bought a bike when his first salary was credited and a luxury car within the next six months. He was then getting a take-home salary of ₹30,000 and was comfortable paying an EMI of ₹15,000. Sunil became eligible for a home loan from the company in 2012, and he bought a house for ₹36,00,000. Sunil was unstoppable! He is now a manager, earning an annual package of ₹22,00,000 and heading a department at BHEL.

Somnath had different plans. He didn't buy a bike or a car as he already owned a bike. He took a home loan from the bank and bought a house in 2009 for ₹22,00,000 on an EMI. In 2013, when Sunil was buying his first house, Somnath sold off this house for ₹50,00,000 and bought a bungalow for ₹76,00,000 in a posh locality. Somnath left BHEL in 2013 to start his entrepreneurial journey and he now owns the largest financial consultancy in the state with an AUM of ₹50,00,00,000. Other than a financial consultancy, Somnath has built several other businesses, most of which are doing well.

Do you wonder how their fate was so similar yet so different? I don't deny fate's hand here because getting a huge income is your fate. It's uncertain and largely out of your control because of several external factors—from a small conflict with the boss to an economic crisis. However, how efficiently you use your money is a skill and is certainly in your control. The decision to buy, spend, and save is mostly with you. If the income side of the money equation is defined by fate, the expense side of the equation is largely defined by your habits and decisions.

Remember that wealth is created only by accumulating the leftover income after spending. While there are chances one can become wealthy without a high income, it is impossible without lower spending.

Sunil focused on spending money on assets that depreciated the moment they left the showroom. At the same time, Somnath's focus was on saving money, spending less, and creating wealth. He invested the leftovers in real estate always appreciates, creating wealth. Though both Somnath and Sunil were qualified financial professionals, their approach to financial wellness was poles apart. After all, wisdom does not come from qualification alone.

Self-Reflection

Think carefully and answer these simple questions to assess your financial wellness: How prepared are you to handle unexpected expenses? Are constantly rising prices forcing you to change your lifestyle? Does market volatility impact your temperament? What's your outlook towards your financial future? Do you follow any financial routines or habits? What financial habits did you form or change in the last year? Which of your financial decisions made in the past are you most proud of? How effectively are you meeting your long-term and short-term financial goals? What is your next long-term goal?

Financial Self-Care

The period of extended lockdown was hard-hitting for most of us—physical, mental, intellectual, social, occupational, and financial wellness were all disturbed. Since then, many of us have reassessed our wellness and prioritised self-care. Yet surprisingly, financial wellness is still commonly overlooked.

It is so because people often believe that financial well-being solely entails having a substantial amount of money. However, it extends beyond mere wealth accumulation to encompass freedom from financial worries and stress, navigating through challenges and uncertainties, and learning from financial mistakes.

However, financial wellness is the relationship with your economic and financial resources, including how you handle your finances. It involves the knowledge of achieving your financial goals, having a clear strategy to navigate rocky patches, and building a solid foundation and understanding to practice financial self-care. Financial self-care generates awareness about your current status and desired destination, boosting confidence in your ability to handle any uncertainties. This means that you are aware of but not intimidated by the risk and can endure setbacks. It is also about figuring out how a financial plan fits into your life to achieve holistic wellness and happiness.

How do you know whether you are stuck or doing fine? What are the areas for improvement in your financial wellness?

There are five indicators of financial wellness:

i. You have an adequate emergency fund.
ii. You spend every penny mindfully to achieve your financial goals.
iii. You are confident and make your financial decisions yourself.
iv. You have set your financial goals and daily move closer to them.
v. Money is not a cause of stress to you, as you are in control of your future financial needs.

Financial self-care can prevent obstacles in pursuing your dreams, allowing the flexibility to follow them and make the best of the opportunities. The road to financial wellness starts with financial literacy. Though it is always better to start early, there is no age for financial literacy. You can start when you feel it's the right time for you. Being literate means knowing where you are, what you have, and where you want to be. It is the knowledge of what and how you earn and where you spend. A sustainable financial foundation and literacy revolves around four psychological aspects—focus, patience, objectivity, and motivation.

Focus provides the direction, speed, and determination to achieve the goal. Ask yourself whether you have SMART financial goals. Do you know how to get there? Are you working towards these goals? Are you aware of your progress? Are you motivated to pursue them?

Patience provides composure; one waits for the fruit to ripen, keeps moving according to the plan, trusts oneself and one's financial decisions, and remains optimistic and confident of the result. Ask yourself if you stick to your financial goals and decisions and stay calm during financial emergencies and market volatility. How easily do you adapt to the changing demands of the situation?

Objectivity helps make the right choices and take the right actions. Note if your investments are diversified. What do you prefer more, saving or spending? What do you focus on, risk or return?

Motivation to create a plan is achieved when you have a vision for your financial future. Reflect upon the reason behind seeking financial wellness—is it for safe retirement, financial independence, or wealth creation?

Mantras to Achieve Financial Wellness

1. Create a Budget: When you see those figures in black and white in front of you, it can make a huge difference. Creating a budget can help you track your income and expenses. You'll be able to see where you are overspending, how you can save, and what is your surplus. Tracking your income and expenses regularly can improve your focus and objectivity and motivate you to build financial health.
2. Conduct a Financial Audit: Once you have the figures in front of you, learn about your financial habits. Do your financial audit—what is essential, what's not, what are your

economic aspirations and values, where and how you will invest, what are your financial priorities, how and what can be improved, and where are the opportunities to save or spend less.

3. Define Your Financial Success: Everyone has different aspirations and values in life, so success looks different for all of us. Define clearly what financial success means to you in the context of your life.
4. Set SMART Financial Goals: Set Specific, Measurable, Achievable, Realistic, and Time-Bound (SMART) financial goals that can encourage you and keep you on track for your desired lifestyle. Write them all down in your journal and prioritise them—children's education, buying a house, a trip abroad, financial independence, early retirement, wealth creation, charity, stability, etc.
5. Make Your Financial Decisions: What is your plan to achieve your goals? What is your strategy to earn, save, invest, and spend? Do you plan to earn more, spend less, and invest right to build your financial health? How will you manage the risks and uncertainties? Create a financial to-do list.
6. Set up an Emergency Fund: To be in control of your life, set up an emergency fund and top it up every month till you reach your target. When you know what constitutes an emergency for you, you can better specify your target. In principle, emergency funds equal 3–6 months of household income to protect yourself from most crises.
7. Get Insured: Secure yourself from huge and unexpected expenses and losses with adequate insurance. Although term life insurance and medical insurance are most desirable for everyone, vehicle insurance is mandatory

by law. Home insurance and business insurance are also recommended.

8. Invest Your Savings: Strike a healthy balance of earning-spending, saving-investing, risk-returns, and present-future to achieve financial wellness. Invest your savings wisely and regularly—for a minimum of five years if you're new to investing. Diversify your investments to get optimum growth potential by mitigating market volatility.
9. Be Patient: In the game of investing, the power of compounding is a game changer. Don't panic, be patient, and stay invested through the thick and thin of the market. Wait to reap the rewards.
10. Reduce Debt: Eliminating debt is impossible, mainly for the middle-income group, but we can always aim to reduce it. EMIs leave you with fewer savings and investments and slim chances of growing your wealth.
11. Tap into Available Resources and Tools: Take advantage of benefits offered by your employer, i.e., provident fund, gratuity, and retirement benefits, where you can invest along with the employer's share. Doing so can bring you threefold benefits: First, you save money before it even reaches you. Second, your money is invested in a smart instrument. And third, you receive tax benefits on most such investments. Take advantage of the tax benefits offered by the government. Plan your investment and taxes strategically to get maximum benefits.
12. Get Help: Discuss your finances with a financial advisor, who can then plan the investments that meet your financial goals, save tax, and provide security, along with a cushion for the rainy days.

Other than the above-mentioned mantras, here are a few ground rules for financial wellness:

a. Start investing early. Even if it is a small sum, make it a habit and keep thinking with a long-term horizon in mind.
b. Avoid high-interest debts. Avoid zero-percent financing schemes.
c. Use credit cards sparingly and always pay the total outstanding amount.
d. Spend responsibly. Be frugal.
e. Start a side hustle or create passive income sources to increase your earnings.
f. Car loan EMI should not exceed 10–15 per cent of your post-tax monthly income. The cost of the car should not be over 60 per cent of your annual income.
g. Do not confuse luxuries with necessities. Track your post-spending emotions and eliminate spending that makes you feel guilty. For instance, eating out every day is undoubtedly a luxury.
h. Savings, investment, and insurance are three distinct things that offer protection, wealth, and security, respectively. Don't treat them as one.
i. Always involve your life partner and other family members in financial planning.
j. Spend on your financial education.

Financial wellness is unique for each one of us, and so is our approach towards it. Whatever your method is, always keep a holistic outlook to harness your strengths and tap into the available opportunities. Keep in mind that financial wellness is about effectively managing the sail in the storm and enjoying the sail in the calm seas.

SUPERPOWER 36

FRUGALITY

Waste No More

'He who will not economise will have to agonise.'
—Confucius

I did not deliberately start my journey to frugal living. Instead, it began when I was completely overwhelmed. I was working in a stable nine-to-five job, earning reasonably well, and was one of the top four at my organisation. I was still not satisfied. It felt like something was amiss, but I was not sure what that was. For quite some time, I believed I was not making any difference in the world. Why talk about the world when I was not making a difference in my own? When I was not doing the things that I wanted to do, what right did I have to talk about the world? Then, just like that, one fine day, I decided to leave this stable job for my entrepreneurial aspirations.

I registered my company, rented a single-room office space in the city's commercial hub, and started my coaching, training, and consulting business. I was minimalistic in my approach. I invested my entire emergency fund, which equalled my six-month salary, to run this business. Income was uncertain, and the expenses were as certain as they could get. I also had additional fixed costs associated with running a full-fledged office. Although my supportive husband took complete care of my personal and household expenses, I was still overwhelmed. This was when I started practising self-imposed frugal living.

It was quite an experience! My house was organised but every bit of it was loaded with a lot of unused things like clothes, shoes, make-up, imitation jewellery, kitchen and toilet supplies, gadgets, equipment, and much more.

The first step of my frugal journey was decluttering. Everything I didn't use, need, or love was to go away—either binned or donated. Surprisingly, alongside the physical space, my mental space also decluttered in the process. I had much more time, energy, patience, financial freedom, and wisdom to spend money on my priorities.

To this day, every time I do a round of decluttering, I still find things I don't use, need, or love anymore. Every round reminds me of my pledge to ask myself 'why' instead of 'what' before any purchase. Now, my family only buys things we need, use, and love, and not because the items are on sale. Every round was a realisation that we have paid a fortune to learn that a bargain is only a rip-off if we don't use the things we buy. This does not mean we are stifling our desires; it simply signifies that we are just not wasting money, time, or energy.

Self-Reflection

Take a walk around your house and inspect every corner. Then, list the things, clothes, shoes, gadgets, equipment, or anything else that you haven't used for over a year. Reflect on how much money you spent on these items and the time, energy, and money you spent on their maintenance. Jot these items down in your Evolve Journal.

Frugality Is a Mindset

Frugality is not about being cheap and stingy, but rather about using resources mindfully and getting the best value from spending. Being frugal can be challenging, but it was a way of life for our ancestors. Our lifestyle and mindset gradually changed with the growth of industrialisation and consumerism, so much so that being thrifty is now looked down upon.

Famous author Yuval Noah Harari has written about this in his book *Sapiens: A Brief History of Humankind*, 'Consumerism has worked very hard, with the help of popular psychology ('Just do it!) to convince people that indulgence is good for you, whereas frugality is self-oppression.'

Frugality mindset doesn't ask one to become a miser and not spend at all or enjoy life. Instead, it is the art of knowing where to be economical and where not to compromise so that you can spend without guilt and save without shame. The frugality mindset is an art that the world's wealthiest people like Warren Buffet, Mark Zuckerberg, Bill Gates, Narayan Murthy, and Azim Premji have mastered. The rich have a frugal mindset. They believe in investing money and creating wealth, and the rest of us believe in spending money to simply buy things. One can get money and become wealthy by luck, but only a frugal individual will manage to sustain that wealth.

Frugality is a mindset of being economical. It involves eliminating the waste of food, time, money, and energy. it frees you from consumerism's stronghold.

When you are mindful of your spending, you search for creative ways to get things done, such as reusing things by relying on your imagination. You also become disciplined and organised about your food, time, money, and other resources. The notion of simple living and high thinking will liberate you and make you more resilient to change.

Practising mindful frugality can enrich all other dimensions of wellness. It can assist you in achieving real success and lasting happiness. Anyone open to change can accomplish a wholesome life and genuine happiness, and this frugality mindset can consciously shift your approach to life with consistent practise.

Mantras to Unlock the Frugality Mindset

1. Frugality Is a Relative Term: Frugality can look different to different people, so avoid comparing or imposing your idea of frugality on anyone. Things that look like a luxury to you can be a necessity for another. For instance, I prefer using a reusable cotton towel over disposable tissue paper, whereas not everyone in my family prefers this. Disposable tissue is a necessity for them.
2. Start with Yourself: Spend your resources mindfully, and keep influencing others. They will eventually come on board. When you start early, you stay ahead. Practising mindful frugality can set you apart, so, keep yourself focused on mindful spending, saving, and investing.
3. Focus on the Value: A frugality mindset is not about always saying no. Instead, it is about not falling for instant gratification and focusing on the value you get for what you've spent. It entails focusing on the why. When planning

to eat out with your family, think about your why—is it the taste or do you want to spend quality time with your family? If it's the latter, be creative and think of more productive ways of connecting with them, like cooking together. Similarly, go for a simple watch if your why is to keep time. Go for a smartwatch if you are looking for more. Purchase an expensive watch if your why is status.

4. Think out of the Box: Constraints are the mother of all innovations. When faced with restrictions, you are forced to be creative. Train your brain to think out of the box—with your time, money, and resources. Turn leftover food into something gourmet, give personalised and handmade gifts to friends, etc. These gifts will not only save money but also strengthen your relationship.
5. Exercise Self-Control: Resist impulsive buying. Think twice before any purchase, and question yourself: 'Is it a need or greed?' Self-control is especially recommended for reusable items with a longer life, such as clothes, shoes, gadgets, etc. Sleep on all the purchases that are not an absolute necessity. The desire will vanish when you sleep on it, giving you enough time to assess the product's utility.
6. Be Assertive: Some of the buying decisions are purely emotional. Several people find it difficult to say no to their loved ones. Learn to be assertive, learn to say no without hurting anyone, learn to say what you really wish to say, and don't say yes when you don't want to.
7. Enjoy Small Things: Happiness is a moment—whether you buy a Ferrari or a small car, the happiness of buying a new car will be the same. You'll be excited for a few days, but soon the novelty will wear off. So, it's essential to enjoy little things and real things, like good company, nature,

and the comfort of home. Happiness derived from small things stays forever because it is real.

8. Maintain Discipline: Don't just get up and spend money. Plan your spending, shopping, parties, outings, etc. It may sound boring but, remember, no one has ever achieved success without discipline.
9. Don't Get Carried Away: Don't buy things just because everyone around you is doing so. Focus on your priorities, purpose, and financial wellness.
10. Be Mindful while Using Offers: Offers are psychological games. You spend extra on products you don't need simply because it was on discount! Combo deals often provide you with products that you never needed in the first place. Sometimes, these offers are misleading, too. Once, I went shopping with a friend at a multi-brand wholesale store, and my friend picked up a kitchen tissue roll—a pack of four—selling for ₹207. I checked my options out of curiosity. There was a pack of two selling for ₹111. The pack of four was cheaper, but then I checked the number of tissues per pack. There were 60 tissues for each roll in the pack of two, making it ₹0.90 per tissue, and the pack of four had 50 tissues for each roll costing ₹1.035 per tissue. This is a difference of 15 per cent, which is huge. Always check thoroughly as every bit counts.
11. Practise, Practise, Practise: Frugality goals are not achieved overnight. Go slow and tackle one category at a time. For instance, if you wish to start your frugality journey by not eating out, don't just ban eating out altogether. Instead, aim to reduce the number of times you eat out. Keep at it

and gradually deal with different categories. The key is to keep practising till you reach your target.

The superpower of frugality aims at minimising waste and getting the most out of our resources—time, money, and food. Don't be so miserly that you compromise with the quality of life. Don't opt for inferior products. Simply, reduce your wants.

Find ways to save resources and ensure your decision pays off now and doesn't backfire later. Consider this, a cheap pair of running shoes can damage your knees, making it difficult for you later in life. Focus on the value, not the price. Don't make the cheapest option your default option.

Remember, no amount of resources can make you comfortable until you are sure of what you want. Consider practising mindful frugality by looking at resources as the means to an end, not the end itself. This can lead to a better, more fulfilling, and happy life.

SUPERPOWER
37

CHOICE

Do You Choose to Live by Choice?

'The future depends on what you do in the present.'
—Mahatma Gandhi

An elderly man was narrating a story to his grandson, 'There is an intense fight inside me between two wolves.'

He added, 'One wolf is evil—he is angry, envious, greedy, and arrogant. He is full of guilt and self-pity. He has complexes and bitterness, and he lives in a false ego. He holds many regrets and is always sad and depressed.'

The man continued, 'The other is a good wolf. He is joyous, peace-loving, hopeful, humble, and kind. He is calm and benevolent. He is empathetic, generous, and compassionate. He spreads love and speaks the truth.'

The old man added further, 'This is not my fight alone. This fight is inside everyone, you and me alike.'

The grandson curiously asked his grandfather, 'Dadaji, which wolf will win?'

'The one we feed,' the old man replied.

Self-Reflection

Reflect in your Evolve Journal on the past few days and observe which wolf you are feeding more.

Life Is a Matter of Choice

Destinations are set. We may not have the power over results, but we can certainly mould our memories—memories that are formed when we approach life, memories that are made when we navigate through the thick and thin of life, and memories that are created during the process of living. As it's said, enjoy your journey because the destination may not be as beautiful as you think.

Destinations are determined by numerous factors, of which 99 per cent are beyond our control. The 1 per cent that is in our control is determined by our approach. We can control only this 1 per cent by making the right approach.

However, most of us are so desperate and obsessed with controlling and changing the uncontainable 99 per cent that we often ignore the manageable 1 per cent. At times, when it is not missed, we typically are reluctant to address the only bit in our control. Thus, 99 per cent of life happens and we create the remaining 1 per cent.

Here's a letter that touched my heart.

Dear Madam,

Hope you're doing well! I just wanted to take a moment to tell you how much I appreciate your guidance and support when I was struggling.

I have such a clear memory of when we first met. I was working in a toxic job and had a sense of dissatisfaction with my life. I was so lost and unsure of myself, and I remember you saying, 'Life is all about the choices you make, and only you have the power to control your life and create the change you want to see. Right or wrong is next, but are you ready to make an informed choice for yourself?' This was a game changer.

Thankfully, I trusted you at that time. I was able to get hold of my emotions and tap into my inner wisdom. Listening to my gut, I found the courage to leave my toxic job and start my own business. It's been a journey, but I'm happy and at peace like never before. I know I made the right choice. I owe so much of that to your encouragement and guidance.

I am writing to say thank you from the bottom of my heart. I feel incredibly lucky to have met you and I wish you to be my confidant forever.

Best wishes to you, and may your guidance and support continue to positively impact the lives of others.

Take care,

Ruchi

Whether or not you actively choose, you are still making a choice. Therefore, not making a choice and not moving ahead is not an option. The superpower of choice is not about making a right or a wrong choice; it's in the fact that we have control over our choices. Choices don't guarantee rewards, but they will always leave you with memories and experiences worth revisiting. It is easy to make peace with the outcome when you have made an informed and thoughtful decision and you know that you did your best.

We make choices all day, be it when to wake up and when to sleep. Few choices appear to be life-changing, whereas some others seem inconsequential. Whether life-changing or insignificant, all choices matter. When we decide to change or to maintain the status quo, the first step in this journey of personal evolution is to resolve to use the superpower of choice wisely, ensuring a happy and meaningful life.

Mantras to Unlock the Power of Choice

1. Don't Overload: All choices matter, but do not overload yourself with trivial choices, such as the daily menu or clothes to wear. Overload can overwhelm and suffocate the mind, leaving us exhausted and anxious. Strategise to reduce the options. For instance, make a menu for the entire week and repeat it without overloading the mind, assign colours to the days and wear clothes accordingly.
2. Avoid Delaying: This, again, applies mainly to trivial choices. The more time you take to make a choice, the harder it is to fall into the traps. The longer you take, the more difficult it is to say no, making you think about what you are expected to do instead of what you want to do.
3. Go Slow: Significant choices, especially choices made during a crisis, must be well thought out. Don't make these choices in haste; discuss and contemplate before coming to a decision.
4. Reflect: Determine your values. Self-reflect to remind yourself of your priorities and goals in life, and consider the impact of your choice(s).
5. Never Choose in an Emotional State: Never promise when happy; never decide when hurt. It is advisable to delay

making any decisions until you have gained control over your intense emotions.

6. Listen to Your Gut: Your intuition usually aligns with your true self. Listen to your gut to get out of autopilot mode and make better and more conscious decisions.
7. Consider Alternatives: To make an informed choice, it is essential to consider as many alternatives as possible.
8. Seek Help: Others can offer you unique perspectives that you may not have considered before. Discuss your options with the people you trust.
9. Follow Others: While you will seldom find a perfect fit, follow people who have made the right decisions in similar situations.
10. Let Go: Admit that you cannot control everything. It's better to let go of the things you cannot control for your mental peace.

Act accordingly once you have made your choice. It's now time to get going, but remember that the superpower of choice is *yours*.

SUPERPOWER 38

UNPLUGGING

Do You Unplug to Recharge?

'Almost everything will work again if you unplug it for a few moments, including you.'

—Anne Lamott

I was sitting with my friends at a coffee shop when one of them asked, 'What is your mature bag?' and everyone started laughing. I was blank. Now they were laughing at me.

I was embarrassed for not getting the joke, not being in trend, and being ignorant of a phenomenon so illustrious that everyone but me knew it.

After a moment of embarrassment, I asked, 'I didn't get it! What are you talking about?' They laughed at me again and told me the story of the mature bag. How this video of a 17-year-old got viral, and now he is the talk of the town, and his memes are trending all over. Even the Mumbai police had joined in the trend and circulated messages around it. Companies were giving names to their bags.

I was unaware. Though I experienced FOMO for a short while, I was happy that I was unplugged.

Self-Reflection

Imagine you have missed a trend! How would you react? Will you be embarrassed about missing it? Do you always strive to keep up with the trends? How often do you unplug, other than while you're sleeping? Do you experience FOMO when you unplug? Answer these questions in your Evolve Journal.

Unplug for Mindfulness

These days, the internet dominates our lives. We can do anything, anytime, anywhere if we have internet access. If I ask you to put your phone away, would you? If not, reflect on your daily routine and ask yourself, 'How many times during the day do I check my phone?'

You cannot think of a number because it is too often to count, isn't it? But you are like most people in the world. Still, you must feel uneasy about the fact that, in the pursuit of missing nothing in the virtual world, you are missing out on real-life experiences.

Who is to be blamed? In this fast-paced world of information and communication, we do almost everything and anything on our internet-enabled screens. People meet and greet, pursue hobbies, build businesses, get experiences, do their jobs, realise aspirations, and much more. It is practically impossible to live an unplugged life because most things require the internet. Modern-day websites are also designed in such a way that they keep us hooked. It simply takes a notification on the phone, and just like that, we while away our time on mindless surfing.

If this rings a bell and you want to truly live and enjoy life, there is hope for you. Instead of giving technology a bad name, let us learn to unplug and observe this fast to thrive. We just have to acknowledge and regulate our triggers to make this incredible technology work in our favour.

Mantras to Unlock the Power of Unplugging

1. Know Your Why: The first step to unplugging is to answer: 'Why am I doing this?' 'Why do I fear unplugging?' 'What is my fear: FOMO, hurting others, or lagging behind?' 'Are all these fears real or just in my head?' Once you realise that fear is only your perception and has nothing to do with the real world, it will be easier to unplug. Be conscious about your choice and keep coming back to your 'why' whenever you feel like you're losing touch.
2. Track Your Usage: Install any screen-time tracking app on your phone. You will be surprised to see that most of your screen time is spent on non-productive social media platforms like WhatsApp, Facebook, Twitter, Instagram, etc.
3. Be Selective: The people you choose to surround yourself with have a significant impact on your mindset. The internet is not an exception. Be mindful of the company you keep online as well. Unfollow or mute notifications from people and groups that do not add any value.
4. Know your Triggers: Be mindful of what triggers you. Notifications can distract anyone, and their resolve is simple as well. First, turn off the notifications. Second,

uninstall addictive apps—like games and shopping apps from your device. This doesn't mean you should avoid using them altogether, but rather access them through the browser instead. Third, log out from the mail accounts on your device after work hours. These are merely suggestions and ideas. You can always devise your formula.

5. Set Boundaries: Our boundaries of work and home are blurry, and since a lot of us work from home, these boundaries are further blurred, which makes unplugging very difficult. Whether you work from home or go to the office, clearly set your work and home boundaries. Schedule your work hours, work with complete focus, and unplug after your work hours. You can attend to the e-mails and messages the next day.
6. Start Your Day Right: Begin your day mindfully instead of mindlessly browsing the internet. Do not start your day on your phone. Spend the first hour of your day on self-care activities like exercise, meditation, and nature walks.
7. Get in Touch with Reality: Minimise the consumption of information and entertainment online. Read physical books and newspapers. Spend time with people, family, and friends. Step out of the house and play real games and sports.
8. One Step at a Time: Don't eliminate a lot of technology from your routine altogether. Instead, aim for only a 10 per cent reduction at a time. Keep adding another 10 per cent when you are comfortable without the previous ones.
9. Establish a Technology-Free Zone: Spend quality time with your family in the no-technology zone. Define an area of the house that is free from the usage of technology—it could be the dining area, bedroom, living room, or any

other room. Setting up an area alone will not help until you spend time together daily in that zone.

10. Media Detox: Ancient scriptures advocated several fasts—food, speech, breath, movement, and thoughts—to detox our body and mind and curb vices. I am proposing a modern detox that will help you restrain the modern-day evil. Fasting on media is today's detox. Our minds are excessively occupied with unsolicited information and entertainment, which gets tiring. Fasting on media calms the mind. To observe this fast, keep away from all media, newspapers, television, mobile phones, computers, laptops, etc., for 24 hours. This fast should be observed once a week. Then, observe this fast once a month, and afterwards, switch back to a weekly detox. Take one extended detox every year by observing the media fast for seven days to one month at one stretch. This detox can rest and repair the mind, making it more agile and composed.
11. Create Your Own System: You often need to find out what works for you as you know what works best to break your habits. Other than the above-mentioned measures, here are some more ideas that can get you started:

    Turn your display to grey scales—it turns less attractive

    Remove the social media apps from your home screen

    Set aside time for using social media apps

    Let someone else change your password until your chosen day

    Log out every time you use any app—be it social media, e-mail, or anything else

- Keep your laptop and mobile in another room while eating, watching television, or working
- No TV in the bedroom and no mobile on the bed

Unplug for better productivity and focus, better sleep, a calm and healthy mind, better relationships, and improved health. Unplugging is essential for generating positivity and developing your superpowers. Unplug to become a better person. Unplug for your well-being. Unplug for any reason, but make sure to do so now and then.

SUPERPOWER 39

CHANGE

Do You Change before You Have To?

'The only constant in life is change.'

—Heraclitus

One day, a man fell into a river. The bystanders started panicking and shouting for help. People wanted to assist the man but they couldn't because of the strong current. The man drifted away to a dangerous waterfall.

One onlooker exclaimed, 'He is gone! Only a miracle can save him now.'

The man fell down the waterfall. However, miraculously, he reached the bottom unharmed. People were amazed and asked how he was able to survive.

The man smiled, and said, 'I adapted with the water; I allowed it to take charge. I came out with the swirl after spinning with the tide. I survived because I did not resist.'

Self-Reflection

Reflect on a few recent changes you have made in your life, such as remote learning, etc. Take note of your behaviour and reactions in your Evolve Journal.

Were you proactive in changing yourself? Have you improved your abilities to better accommodate the change? Did you take any other steps that helped you cope better? What did you resist the most?

Change to Remain

Who would have thought that my decision to become a trainer and coach would lead to such an incredible personal journey? When I look back at all the changes and transformations I have embraced, I can't help but feel amazed. From completing my PhD in finance to pursuing psychology and taking up coaching as a career, from leaving my job to starting my own business, I've learnt so much, which has led to immense growth. I even lost a lot of weight and cut my hair along the way—talk about a complete evolution, right?

But what's even more incredible is that I've had the honour of working with some remarkable people over the years. Whether they were struggling in their careers, relationships, health, finances, or simply seeking personal growth and transformation, each individual's journey has been unique and inspiring.

I have noticed that those who were able to achieve their goals and succeed had something in common—they were willing to leave their comfort zones and embrace change. They knew the journey wouldn't be easy, but they were determined to take risks and try new things. It was inspiring to see them gaining better self-awareness through listening to themselves and others, reflecting on their experiences, making conscious choices, embracing change, practising new skills, and learning from their mistakes. In the end, they were able to achieve their goals, build stronger relationships, and find a sense of purpose and fulfilment in their lives.

Of course, the road to transformation is full of twists and turns, and it requires enormous courage and determination. It's completely normal to feel scared to take that leap of faith, especially when you're unsure of what lies ahead. That's why having someone to guide and support you can make all the difference.

I have seen firsthand how a little bit of guidance and support can help people achieve their goals. Whether it's the one who was feeling stuck in a dead-end job or someone who was struggling with a difficult relationship, stepping out of their comfort zone was ultimately what led to success.

In the end, there's nothing more rewarding than seeing my clients evolve, achieve their goals, build stronger relationships, and find a sense of purpose and fulfilment in their lives. It's a reminder that change is never easy, but with the right mindset, support, and guidance, it's always possible.

Change is the only constant. Since birth, we have been changing, just as the world around us. As they say, you cannot step on the same river twice. As much as change is a constant, so is this fear of change. Humans strive for a predictable and routine life. Divorce and suicide rates around the world rose during the lockdown in 2020. This fact made me write this book.

This fear of change can affect people in myriad ways. Excessive fear can turn into a phobia—people can feel helpless as if they have no control over their lives. They want to live in their past, believing they have control over it. Such people find it difficult to progress with time, leading to stagnation. This, in turn, leads to depression, which affects them in every facet of their lives, such as health, relationships, career, finances, etc.

The power to change is the superpower that differentiates the winners from the also-rans. The one who changes quickly is the winner; others follow suit. Not changing is not an option at all. You can either change with time, or time will change you.

Change can be summarised in two words: Adaptability and flexibility. These words are often used interchangeably. Both terms mean changing oneself. Adaptability is focused on hardcore, long-term changes, which focus on modifying and adjusting ideas and perceptions. Flexibility is the ability to adjust to sudden, short-term changes and to accommodate others' needs. For instance, one needs to adapt when getting married, moving to a new city, to be flexible to change the side of the bed one sleeps in or to change the reporting time at work. Nevertheless, the ideas discussed here apply to both adaptability and flexibility.

Those who display the power of change are preferred everywhere, as they are willing to adapt to new ideas and innovations. They are eager to learn new skills and behaviours quickly in response to the changing environment. They are flexible to the needs of others and accommodate its volatile nature. Flexible individuals effectively respond to circumstances and are preferred as leaders, teammates, or partners.

Mantras to Unlock the Power of Change

1. Be Open-Minded: Embrace and look forward to changing. Take risks and accept the results. Change is never easy, so practice self-care during complex changes and, when needed, reach out for help.
2. Be Self-Aware: People can change only when they are aware of their shortcomings. Strive to be mindful of the gaps or the places you lack. Self-awareness should always be accompanied by self-belief. Awareness without a belief system can be demotivating—you know that you are lacking but also that you are not capable of overcoming it. On the other hand, when you are overconfident but unaware, you miss an opportunity for improvement.
3. Learn from Failure: You learn from challenges by focusing on improving instead of proving yourself. Challenges and failures show us successful ways of approaching a problem, learning more, performing better, and minimising failure in the future.
4. Learning, Thinking and Problem-Solving Skills: Reflect and seek feedback on your thought processes. Use the conducive reflections and feedback to learn. Approach a problem systematically, explore the options, select the best-suited alternative, and implement the solution. Think clearly before making decisions.
5. Practise Consciously: Be mindful of the change. Focus on what's happening in the present; forget about the past or future. Deliberately choose to implement new learnings and improve your performance.

6. Leave Your Comfort Zone: Change is always uncomfortable. Practise tweaking your comfort zone with simple things like brushing with your non-dominant hand or taking an unfamiliar route to work. This can prepare you for the inevitable uncomfortable circumstances, making you comfortable stepping out of the box. Furthermore, it also boosts creativity and flexibility.

Anyone who rejects change will cease to grow and will not experience progress. You become a better version of yourself when you embrace change. So, don't leave change to mere chance.

SUPERPOWER 40

SELF-DISCOVERY

From What You Are to What You Can Be

I am not in competition with anyone but myself. My goal is to improve myself continuously.'

—Bill Gates

A well-educated and highly successful man once visited a spiritual teacher.

He asked him, 'Guruji, by God's grace, I have everything. Still, I feel incomplete. Please help me.'

As soon as Guruji started speaking, the man interrupted and began discussing his life events.

After listening to his side, Guruji restarted the discourse. The man interrupted again, not allowing Guruji to finish his sentence. This went on for a while. The man kept interrupting Guruji frequently and interjecting his beliefs during the discourse.

Suddenly, Guruji stopped, and said, 'Let's take a small break.'

Guruji then invited the man to his cottage for tea. Guruji poured the tea into the mug and kept pouring it even after the mug was full, causing it to overflow.

The man exclaimed, 'Guruji, stop! The mug is already full.'

Guruji looked at the man, smiled and said, 'This mug is you, my child, so full of yourself that you don't listen. I cannot help you until you make some room in your mug to receive.'

Self-Reflection

Introspect and ask yourself: Am I ready? What is my why? Who am I competing with?

Your Self Is Worth Discovering

Life moves fast. Our minds are preoccupied with many thoughts about our responsibilities, commitments, expectations, competition, love, life, work, and several other questions. Thinking about the 'self' is the last thing that occurs to us. We seldom think about 'Who are we?' 'What are we capable of?' 'What is our purpose in life?' 'Where are we going?' 'What do we want from life?' We are so occupied with others and other things that we miss discovering our authentic selves.

If you are in the same boat and wondering how and where to start the journey towards the self, know that the first step is to understand that you are your only competition. When you compete with others, your life revolves around them. Likewise, when you compete with yourself, your life revolves around your own self. Self-competition ensures a better version of yourself.

Understanding the competition is the prerequisite to competing. Reflect, introspect, and answer some basic questions before you commence your journey of self-discovery and self-improvement. What makes you happy? What makes you sad? What do you enjoy doing? What do you hate? What do you want to achieve (your destination)? Where are you today (your starting point)?

Have you heard the story of a lion cub that was raised by a sheep?

> A pregnant lion died soon after giving birth. A mother sheep who witnessed the birth decided to rear the lion cub with her other babies. Growing up with sheep, the cub started thinking and acting like sheep. The cub could never understand why other sheep were making fun of him, why he was so different, looked different, and sounded different. He could sense that he did not belong there, but he was not able to put a finger on the why. Once, another lion noticed this cub running for his life with the herd of sheep. He stopped chasing the sheep and pounced on the young lion. The cub was shaking in fear, and pleaded, 'Please let me go. Please don't eat me. I am just a lamb.' The older lion was surprised and said, 'No, you are a lion, just like me.' But the young one was not convinced, so the older lion took him to a riverbank and showed him their reflection in the water. The cub was thrilled to discover his real self and roared in excitement. Everything changed after that. The birds flew away, the sheep started running away, and they never made fun of him.

This happens to most of us. We consider ourselves one in the crowd until we realise our talents, skills, and superpowers. This realisation is often the result of self-discovery, which can be triggered by a series of events. For the young lion, the process of self-discovery started with the sheep making fun of him, creating a social void, and then encountering the older lion.

Our superpowers are hidden underneath. We discover, we improve, and we evolve on the journey of self-discovery and self-improvement. Self-discovery, improvement, transformation, and evolution do not take place right away. Becoming a better version of oneself is an ongoing process. It's not the destination that matters, but the journey of self-discovery that is truly beautiful and rewarding.

Mantras to Unlock Self-Discovery

1. Maintain a Journal: Journal every day to discover yourself. Write down your goals, dreams, and ups and downs. Journal what you like and dislike, what you want and what you want to get rid of. Pen down all your experiences in this journey. Journal the changes in your life during this journey—your thoughts and gratitude.
2. Practise Visualisation: Set aside time to practise visualisation if journalling is not your cup of tea. Imagine your ideal life, your lifestyle, and your ideal self. Visualise your goals, dreams, ups and downs. Envisage what you want and what you do not. Visualise what you love, what you like, your interests, and your passion. Envision the changes you experience in your evolve journey.
3. Set Relationship Boundaries: The idea is to get rid of toxicity in relationships. Ask yourself if you are being taken for granted, if you feel unwanted, if you feel uneasy in relationships. Honestly assess and be brave in setting boundaries for any toxic relationship(s). Decide who gets a share of your time because not everyone deserves it.
4. Establish a Mindfulness Routine: Engage in some mindfulness routines—meditation, yoga, etc. These

practices can help you conquer negative thoughts and show you the bright and clear path of self-discovery.

5. Leave Your Comfort Zone: Self-discovery is a process of change and change is always uncomfortable. Be prepared to leave your comfort zone and embrace change. Try new things, and you will discover yourself by trial and error.
6. It's Not about Others: Self-discovery is about knowing what you want to be, how you want to see yourself, and not meeting others' expectations. Let go of the expectations others have for you, and release their image of you. Instead, find your North Star. What do you expect from yourself? How do you envision your ideal self?
7. Ask Questions: Asking questions to yourself will help you discover your true self. Ask what makes you happy, what your values are, what brings you joy, what success looks like for you, what gives you satisfaction, and what you fear. Ask as many questions as you can and try finding answers to them.
8. Be Conscious: Self-discovery takes place when you are conscious of yourself and your surroundings. Stay conscious and aware of changes happening within and around you.
9. Empower Yourself: Strengthen and empower yourself on all eight dimensions of wellness—physical, emotional, social, intellectual, environmental, spiritual, and vocational.
10. Seek Help: If you are unsure, ask for help from your friends and family. Discuss why you are unsure of your progress and the reasons for your need for validation or encouragement. Seek help by reading books, articles, and journals. Ask for guidance from a coach if you are uncertain about the path.

Self-discovery is the best journey you can embark upon. I set out to discover myself a few years ago post a year-long contemplation. I had to persuade myself repeatedly by saying, 'Self-care is not a sin.'

HERE'S TO YOUR EVOLUTION

I enjoyed spending time alone back then as well but falsely believed that thinking about the self is selfish. I was a person who could not help being involved with the lives of people around me. I always had to be present for everyone, no matter what was happening around me. Thus, I started ignoring myself and my priorities and putting others first.

I was doing well in my career, but the confines of that job were limiting me. I was good with people, but their attachment was paralysing me. I was successful and happy, but I was yearning for meaning in my life. This was when I started my 'evolve journey' of self-discovery.

My first conscious effort towards self-discovery was setting boundaries in relationships. I consciously started prioritising myself. I was meditating, reflecting, exercising, and eating intentionally. I was spending quality time with my family and friends. I started expressing my feelings in a gratitude journal. I incorporated thought manifestation and affirmations into my routine as well.

I had my doubts, as it was not an easy journey. Even though there were moments of fear and insecurity, knowing myself and unlocking these 40 superpowers sharpened my edge. In this journey of self-discovery, I found myself getting closer to my 'why' every day. This quest of understanding the self has given meaning to my journey with a side of happiness and success. This path of self-discovery has enabled me to help hundreds of souls. I can help generate awareness and curiosity amongst countless others because I know what they are going through when they are feeling intense emotions. I am still discovering myself, as it is a lifelong journey. I wish and hope this book will continue helping people even when I am gone.

If you are a sceptic, I propose you try to not just exist but evolve regardless. Discover yourself because you are worth it.

Supercharge Your Destiny is a book that helps readers build more awareness in order to create meaning, success, happiness, and value in their lives. This book teaches 40 different superpowers that can help them improve their lives and reach their full potential.

For now, I have only shared these 40 superpowers because the journey to evolve holistically can be equated to running a marathon. If you run quickly in the first half, you won't have enough energy left to finish it. These 40 superpowers will put you on track and prepare you not only to participate but also to finish the marathon. As you know, marathon runners often graduate to try triathlons. Your evolved version will look towards upping the ante. With this book, I equip you with your offence strategy—the strengths within you. There's a lot more to learn and I will be expanding on the specifics in future books. More specifically, I will teach you to play defence by conquering the weaknesses within you. For instance, making an effective to-do-list and 5-minute-miracle to combat procrastination.

By practising these skills, readers can learn to live more intentionally and create a life that is meaningful and fulfilling. Overall, this book is a valuable resource for anyone looking to make positive changes in their life and become their best selves.

This journey of self-transformation and evolution is a continuous attempt to get closer to what you can be and find your Ikigai by consciously comprehending answers to these four questions:

What do you love?
What are you good at?
What does the world need?
What can you get paid for?

The best time to plant a tree was 20 years ago. The next best is now. This journey can be overwhelming, so start with one step at a time. These superpowers are your gifts from God. You just need to keep unwrapping, discovering, improving, and practising them. Just like that massive tree that was once a tiny seed, trust yourself, trust the divine, and keep nurturing your superpowers to reap the sweet fruits of success and happiness.

I wish you love and luck on your journey to evolve, and not just exist.

BIBLIOGRAPHY

Aaker, Jennifer L., and Naomi Bagdonas. *Humour, Seriously: Why Humour is a Superpower at Work and in Life, and how Anyone Can Harness It. Even You.* New York: Penguin Business, 2020.

Adams, George M. *You Can.* New Delhi: Fingerprint! Publishing, 2020.

Autobiography of a Yogi (Hindi Pocket Edition). Kolkata: Yogoda Satsang Society of India, 2006.

Bansal, Rashmi. *Stay Hungry, Stay Foolish: The Inspiring Stories of 25 IIM Ahmedabad Graduates who Chose to Tread a Path of Their Making.* Ahmedabad: IIM Ahmedabad, 2008.

Bono, Edward D. *Lateral Thinking: A Textbook of Creativity.* New York: Penguin Adult, 2010.

Browne, Steve. *HR on Purpose: Developing Deliberate People Passion.* Virginia: Society for Human Resource Management, 2017.

Byrne, Rhonda. *The Secret.* New York: Simon & Schuster, 2006.

Carnegie, Dale. *How to Win Friends and Influence People.*: New York: Simon & Schuster, 1998.

Cawthorn, Sam. *Bounce Forward: How to Transform Crisis into Success.* India: John Wiley & Sons Inc, 2013.

Chapman, Gary. *Love is a Verb: Stories of What Happens When Love Comes Alive.* Minnesota: Bethany House Publishers, 2010.

Clear, James. *Tiny Changes, Remarkable Results: Atomic Habits.* New York: Penguin Random House, 2018.

Collins, Jim, and James C. Collins. *Good to Great: Why Some Companies Make the Leap . . . and Others Don't*. New York: HarperCollins, 2001.

Connellan, Tom. *The 1% Solution- for Work and Life*. India: Bhopal: Manjul Publishing House, 2016.

Davis, Martha, Patrick Fanning, and Matthew McKay. *Messages: The Communication Skills Book*. Oakland: New Harbinger Publications, 2009.

De Bono, Edward. *Simplicity*. New York: Penguin, 2009.

De Bono, Edward. *Six Thinking Hats*. New York: Penguin, 2010.

De Bono, Edward. *Teach Yourself to Think*. New York: Penguin Books, 2009.

Dobelli, Rolf. *The Art of Thinking Clearly*. Translated by Nicky Griffin. London: Sceptre, 2013.

Foster, Jack. *How to Get Ideas*. New York: HarperCollins, 2012.

Gandhi, Deepak. *Poor Little Rich Slum*. Delhi: Westland, 2012.

Garg, Ankush, and Ravi Valluri. *The Infinite Mind*. India: Notion Press, 2018.

Goldsmith, Marshall. *What Got You Here Won't Get You There: How Successful People Become Even More Successful*. London: Profile Books, 2008.

Gordon, James S. *Unstuck: Your Guide to The Seven-Stage*. New York: Penguin, 2011.

Harari, Yuval N. *21 Lessons for the 21st Century*. London: Jonathan Cape, 2018.

Harari, Yuval N. *Sapiens: A Brief History of Humankind*. New York: Vintage Books, 2015.

Hill, Napoleon. *Think & Grow Rich*. New Delhi: Fingerprint! Publishing, 2022.

Hinton, Anthony Ray. 'I Spent 28 Years on Death Row.' *The Guardian*, October 21, 2016. Accessed April 8, 2024. https://www.theguardian.com/lifeandstyle/2016/oct/21/28-years-on-death-row.

Housel, Morgan. *The Psychology of Money*. Mumbai: Jaico Publishing House, 2020.

Kakar, Sudhir, ed. *Seriously Strange: Thinking Anew about Psychical Experiences.* New York: Penguin, 2012.

Kalam, A. P. J. Abdul. *Turning Points: A Journey Through Challenges.* Delhi: HarperCollins India, 2012.

Krznaric, Roman, and The School of Life. *How to Find Fulfilling Work.* London: Pan Macmillan, 2012.

McLaren, Karla. *The Language of Emotions: What Your Feelings Are Trying to Tell You.* Boulder: Sounds True, 2010.

Miralles, Francesc, and Héctor García. *Ikigai: The Japanese Secret to a Long and Happy Life.*: New York: Hutchinson, 2017.

Murphy, Joseph. *Believe In Yourself.* Bhopal: Manjul Publishing House, 2014.

Murphy, Joseph. *The Power of Your Subconscious Mind.*: Mumbai: Amazing Reads, 2015.

Papasan, Jay, and Gary Keller. *The One Thing: The Surprisingly Simple Truth Behind Extraordinary Results.* London: Hodder & Stoughton, 2013.

Pease, Allan, and Barbara Pease. *Why Men Don't Listen & Women Can't Read Maps.* Bhopal: Manjul Publishing House, 2006.

Purdy, Michael, and Deborah Borisoff, eds. *Listening in Everyday Life: A Personal and Professional Approach.* Maryland: University Press of America, 1997.

Ranganathan, Sukumar, ed. *The New Age Entrepreneurs*. New Delhi: Random House India, 2012.

Roy, Sumita. *Managing Stress.* Delhi: Sterling Publishers Pvt. Ltd., 2013.

Sharma, Robin S. *The 5 AM Club: Own Your Morning. Elevate Your Life.* Mumbai: Jaico Publishing House, 2018.

Sharma, Robin S. *The Mastery Manual.* Mumbai: Jaico Publishing House, 2015.

Shetty, Jay. *8 Rules of Love.* London: Thorsons, 2023.

Swami, Om. *The Book of Kindness: How to Make Others Happy and Be Happy Yourself.* New York: HarperCollins, 2019.

Tiwari, Payal G. *From XL to XS.* New Delhi: Random House India, 2018.

Tracy, Brian. *Maximum Achievement.* Bhopal: Manjul Publishing House Pvt Limited, 2010.

Vas, Luis S. *Skills for Excellence.* Delhi: Pustak Mahal, 1999.

Vickie L. Milazzo, RN. *Inside Every Woman.* India: John Wiley & Sons Inc, 2010.

Watkins, Philip C. *Gratitude and the Good Life: Toward a Psychology of Appreciation.* Germany: Springer, 2013.

Watson, Stephanie. 'Caffeine and a Healthy Diet May Boost Memory, Thinking Skills; Alcohol's Effect Uncertain.' *Harvard Health Publishing*, 18 June 2014. https://www.health.harvard.edu/blog/caffeine-healthy-diet-may-boost-memory-thinking-skills-alcohols-effect-uncertain-201406187219.

Wood, Alex M., Alex Linley, and Stephen Joseph. 'Gratitude – Parent of all virtues.' *The Psychologist* 20, no. I (January 2007): 18–21.